Three Days For The Rest Of My Life

Robin Barnes

Copyright © 2014 Robin Barnes

K PEPPER PUBLISHING

All rights reserved.

ISBN-13: 978-0692256947

ISBN-10: 0692256946

Dedicated To My Family
and
Sis. Carolyn Robinson

CONTENTS

	Preface	i
	Introduction	viii
Chapter 1	The Gateway	1
Chapter 2	The Ripley's Hook-Up	10
Chapter 3	The Chicken Coop	22
Chapter 4	On A Mission	35
Chapter 5	Big Moosie	40
Chapter 6	The Ride	52
Chapter 7	Choices	65
Chapter 8	The Fig Tree	77
Chapter 9	Blowing Smoke	84
Chapter 10	Three Days For The Rest Of My Life	95

Preface

I grew up in a wonderful home with two loving parents. My father was a dedicated man who put his teachings of the Lord's words into action. By sharing the love of God, he brought clarity and understanding to a lost community.

My father was a retired naval officer. He was an electrician during the time when most blacks in the military were only allowed to become cooks. It was there he learned how electrical circuits functioned together. And I believe that it was from that experience, he later learned how people should function together. He was best known as Police Chaplain WB Barnes. He helped to establish the Chaplaincy Program at the Fairfield County Jail in California.

He was well known by the Vallejo Police Department as demonstrated when he would go on a "ride along" with the Department. It was during those times when my father would come into contact with people from different cultures and diversities; his role as Police Chaplain allowed him a firsthand opportunity to comfort those in need. Many nights my father would receive a phone call from the police department because someone's family had been involved in a tragedy. My father gave compassion and direction to those in need. These are the same qualities that he has given to each member of our family.

My father passed away on September 29, 2007 from a "Glioma" Brain Tumor. During his illness family, members from our church, and many friends from law enforcement and the prison system held my father's condition in prayer unto the Most High God; The Creator of Heaven and earth. Through all of our prayers the Lord felt that it was time to call my father home.

Before my father passed away I had the opportunity to read a letter that I had written to him. It's titled: "A Letter to My Dad."

"Whenever I think of good times or when I find myself in need of encouragement, I will think of you dad. When we come together as a family and bow our heads in prayer I will hear your voice in my heart speaking words of hope.

Throughout my life I think back on the many encouraging words that you have spoken to me. If I were to take them all and place them into a notebook, I could not find one large enough to contain them all.

You are my dad, you are my father, and you are my teacher. I thank you for the many times that I would pick up the telephone after spending hours searching through God's words for understanding. Whether for clarity or confirmation, you have always been able to help me further my understanding.

You have played a major role, by example of the way that we should live our life if we say that we love the Lord. I know that I have the tools to continue down the right path. I will always keep God in my heart, and I will always do my best to live the life of a servant of God.

Through your teaching of God's Word, you have shown me that all things are possible.

PREFACE

When I look at you, I see a man who endures through all circumstances who serves the Lord with gladness. Who enters into battle fully prepared and fights until the end.

Dad, know that I will always love you and thoughts of you shall be with me every day. I will speak with you on tomorrow, and I will delight in the sound of your voice. I will say thank you Lord for your many blessings, for your guidance, and your teaching. I will especially say thank you Lord for my dad whom I love very much. I will ask for a healing for a servant of the Lord, and I will bless the name of the Lord forever and ever.

I shall never forget you and how you touched my life. How you have helped to mold me into the person that I am becoming. One day I will get there.

Get up old soldier and keep pressing on. There is still one more battle to fight.

But if it is time to lay down your sword then the Lord shall set those things in order. But if it is His will that you should carry on then press on dad, press on. Remember we live by faith and not by sight.

I pray that your pain is bearable; your joy is high above the clouds; that your mind is set on things above. That you delight in your surroundings, because your family is here. We are by your side because you mean so much to us. Dad I know that your body is weak right now and things seem a little bleak. But let's go one more inning, or the best two out of three. Let's fight a little bit more. Remember the Great Doctor of all.

Let's ask the Lord for a miracle. The doctors don't know everything, but to God you mean everything, and to us you are everything. We love you still"

My dad fought his illness with dignity, gladness, and faith. We know that to be absent from the body is to be present with the Lord.

Therefore faith overcame denial; as denial turned into acceptance; and acceptance answered my question. Why did my dad have to die?

We are all God's children. He sent His Son for us because He loves us. All we have to do is open our eyes to the things of God. He restored my dad unto Himself in Heaven. He laid down his sword for a crown. I'm going to miss my dad very much, but it would have been selfish to keep him here in pain. I love you dad for always and forever.

I never got a chance to say goodbye to my dad before he passed away even though I was in the room with him. It was my night to stand watch. It was my night to make sure that if my dad needed anything someone would be there. In my mind I asked the question why did I fall asleep when he might have needed me the most. I can only remember a faint noise in the background and I opened my eyes. My son was walking through the door. I looked at my dad and he was gone. Did the Lord protect me from witnessing my dad in such pain? Was he protecting me from having the image in my mind of my dad taking his last breath? Only God knows. All I know is that I let my dad down.

My dad had a DNR (Do not resuscitate order). He didn't want any heroic efforts made to extend his life. But I will never know if he asked for anyone or anything. Goodbye dad, I love you.

My mother is best known as "Mother Barnes." Whether at home, work, or at church, my mother is simply known as "Mother." My mother is a matter of fact person. Whenever she speaks; she means exactly what she says, and says exactly what she means.

My mother has always guided her children with a loving and honest hand. No punishment has ever come undeserving. I remember as a child if we lied or stole "we" knew beyond a shadow of a doubt that we would be punished. Any time we had a problem at school, my mom would always be there taking our side; providing we told her the truth. She always said never have her come to school to defend us in any situation if we have not told her the whole truth. My mother has always provided for us whether emotionally, spiritually, or simply as a mother provides for her children. Growing up I can remember sitting at my mother's feet as she would spend countless moments sharing and teaching us Bible verses and sharing the love of God. She is the best cook that I know. That's why I love Monday's, when the family comes together to eat.

My mom is a Grandmother and a Great-Grandmother. She's earned the right to spoil each of her grandchildren, especially her great-grandchildren as she sees fit. My mom is the pulse of the family, the rhythm and the beat. She's the joy in my heart. It pains me when she is sad. I know that she misses my dad; and I wish that there was something that I could do to change things; but I can't. It's the Lord's doing. We must trust and believe in God's plan of salvation.

My mother retired from Napa State Hospital as a Psychiatric Nurse. Her qualities as a nurse and mother, has gained her great insight into the ability to help her children.

My mother is the president of the "Mother's Board." She sings in both the Mass Choir and the Women's Chorus. She is always on the mission field visiting the sick and shut in, if it's at their home or the hospital, or even on the telephone she shares great words of comfort and of hope. She has the gift of hospitality.

She has a way about herself that places you at ease during your time of need. You can be assured that if you desire someone to find out what's really going on with your illness or you need someone to talk to the doctor on your behalf, my mother will ensure that you are not kept in the dark as she handles things decent and in order.

Prior to my father's illness my mother was diagnosed with Chronic Obstructive Pulmonary Disease (COPD). Her doctor's told her that she may not have much time. The lord had other plans for my mother. My father's condition was a rapid, devastating loss. During his illness my mother's condition seemed to improve. It was as though the Lord allowed her to keep all of her health and strength to take care of my dad.

But I am very much aware that my mother is very sick. Her condition is not improving. But I'm thankful that the Lord is allowing her to continue on. I don't know what I would do without my mother. She is the first person that I call when I get home from work. She is the first person that I call when I need advice.

On May 2, 2009 St. Mark Community Church in Vallejo, California had their annual Mother and Daughter Luncheon. My mom and I were asked to give a short talk. It was an opportunity for me to state in public just how much I love and appreciate my mother while she is yet here.

During my talk, I read a short poem to my mother. It went like this: "A mother is someone who gives her all in all. It takes a special person to be a mother. I don't know about you, but for me there could be no other.
My mother is strong and she is wise, believe me this is no disguise.

She speaks her mind and has even whooped my behind. She taught me right, but I chose wrong. I found my way, because each night she would pray. I thank the Lord for my mother. I thank the Lord that He gave me no other.

Our mothers teach us many things in life. They teach us how to talk and they show us how to walk. Sometimes our strides may falter or we wonder where we are. Some days we look back with surprise that we have come so far.
It is because of our mothers that the world seems a whole lot better. They show us lots of love and give us joy and pleasure. It's no wonder why they are God's treasure." I appreciate my mother, I thank God for her. She is a virtuous woman. She has touched many lives. Most of all she has touched my life. She has always been there for me no matter what type of dirt I found myself in.

I love you mom forever and always.

Introduction

I know firsthand that God answers prayers. He answers prayers through the marvelous work of His Son Jesus Christ, who shed his precious blood on Calvary for a sinner like me. I am a living witness of the unconditional love that God offers. He offers His love both to you and to me.

Growing up in a nurturing environment, as a child my parents showed me the road that I should take, and instilled in me the love of Jesus Christ, even so, one might wonder how my life ended up in such drastic disarray, whereby I took my life and my children's lives for granted. I became homeless and dependent on drugs. It didn't happen overnight; it happened through time. I was in my mid 30's with two children of my own when I became outright defiant and wayward to the message of my youth and decided to stray away

I grew up loving God, but through lack of knowledge I truly didn't fear the Lord, for if I had feared Him as my parents taught me years ago I would have kept His Commandments. Don't get me wrong, I'm not saying that God should be feared in the way that man describes fear. God loves us and He gave His only Begotten Son for us and He created us in His image. Yet we have to understand and realized that there is a spiritual battle going on between satan and the Lord, and unless we recognize the reality of the war, we are going to miss out on the greatest love of all, and we will be destroyed with satan and his little demons.

INTRODUCTION

My mother once gave me a plaque that said, "Age is a high price to pay for maturity." I still have it. I look at it often and wonder where my life could have been if I only understood then, what maturity was all about. When we are young, we think that we have all of the time in the world to get our affairs in order. The world becomes our teacher. Our lessons in life become hard learned. And our life becomes hard lived.

This story is made possible because my family, friends, and members of the Saint Mark Community Church in Vallejo, California, held my wretched soul unto the Most High God in prayer. The Bible says: For the prayer of a righteous man availeth much. If it had not been for a willingness to surrender my situation into the Lord's hands, this story would have never been told because I should have been dead a long time ago.

The lord calls us unto righteousness; He gives us the choice to decide what we want to do with our lives. It was only until I realized that apart from God I can do nothing, but with God all things are possible. I made many attempts to get my life together. A life that I considered to be under control. Each time I tried, I failed. I struggled for many years telling myself and even convincing myself that I could handle my situation on my own. I was too proud, unwilling, and I was insane. I believe that I was insane; because I kept trying to do the same things over and over thinking that each time my circumstances would turn out different and somehow my situation would be fine. To change my condition meant that I had to see myself as I truly was; it meant that I had to look in the mirror, see myself for who I was and who I had become; I wasn't ready to see my true reflection. A mirror tells no lie. It only shows what it sees. I wasn't ready to see the truth.

I convinced myself that if the opportunity to change ever presented itself, I would be unable to succeed and make that change. It was easier to tell myself that I couldn't do it than to actually make an attempt to change. Before my situation changed, I thought that I was doomed to die in my filthy condition. I was tore up from the floor up. I was at a point of no hope. I no longer had the strength to even make the change I so desperately needed. I had spent seven years living in darkness; I was unable and unwilling to turn away from my condition.

But the Lord took a filthy rag like me and dipped my circumstances into His precious blood and made me clean. I have dedicated my life to serving the Lord. Nothing or no one can cause me to turn away from the love of the Lord ever again.

Each time that I reflect on the road of life I chose for myself many years ago when I was living a life filled with guilt and shame, my heart explodes with joy and I begin to cry, for I cannot believe how my life has turned around. I wasn't fit to die, yet I wasn't living. I thank God, because here I am today; no longer lost to a world of habitual dependency clothed in a world of homelessness; no longer estranged from my family.

Because of God's grace and goodness towards me, I must share my story.

Chapter 1

The Gateway

It was the year 1994. I was 35 years old and a single mother of two wonderful children, Christina and John, also known as Tina Tot and John John. I thought my life was under control. After all, I went to work every day. On the weekends I would plan activities with my children. We'd go to the movies, the park, swimming; we did all sorts of activities together. We were living our lives. Life seemed to be going okay. Don't get me wrong; like most people I had my share of problems. Money was tight but we were surviving.

I was a fairly young mom and I still loved to go to the club. I often looked forward to the times when my children would spend the night with family. They were great kids, but come on let's get real, sometimes I needed adult conversation. I did my share of dancing and drinking. I also had my share of hangovers and the like. That comes with the territory, but that didn't keep me from coming home to my children every night.

One weekend my children were staying with relatives. "At last," I said to myself, "since I have a night alone, I think I'll go visit my friend Larry." I knew Larry from work. We had just started seeing each other, just two friends sharing a night together. We were just going to sit around and have a few beers and get to know each other. Little did I know this would be the night that changed my life forever.

We were sitting around talking and drinking, just "Chilling," no big deal or so I thought. I wanted to relax a little bit more. I had brought about "ten cents" worth of hemp (weed) with me, so I decided to pull it out. I'd smoked a little here and there nothing heavy; it was a social remedy for me, a party favor if you will. I'd get about eight or nine Mary Jane sticks (Marijuana) from the whole wop (the whole bag). In all probability the entire package would last me about a month. In those days I told myself that what I was doing was harmless, after all God is the creator of all things and His rain from Heaven cultivated and displayed the splendor of marijuana's proverbial existence in the world for my personal pleasure. Yes God is the Creator of all things; but everything on earth, because of God's Devine Creation has order and purpose. God created gravity as well. My dad always said, "try jumping off of a building and you'll discover just how perfect gravity works."

I used God's Word to justify my evil doings. I told myself that I was different from everyone else who smoked weed because my lifestyle was different. I wasn't hanging out on the street day after day captivated by the folly of a meager existence that held many owners of this product frozen in time to its forbidden pleasures.

I was a weekend worrier just having a little fun. What's the harm in that? I went to work every day. I was able to maintain my job, keep my rent paid, buy groceries and live my life. Anyway my expenditures were only a mere $20 a month. It wasn't like I was taking money from my kids. Little did I know my life was going downhill and I didn't even see the warning signs.

Feeling as though my body was floating on air, I closed my eyes and listened to my mind. I imagined new and refreshing things as I puffed on the weed that I had. My head was above the clouds. I made so many plans in my mind, but none of them ever came to reality.

The truth of the matter is I should have never underestimated sins ability by giving satan freedom to control my flesh from the choices that I made. Smoking weed only created a pattern of destructive behavior, and an atmosphere of endless struggles and disappointments. It gave way to an inner conflict between the flesh and the Spirit of God.

We have to realize that there is a real conflict, a real battle if you will, between the flesh and the Spirit, between satan and the Lord. The desires of our flesh are in a battle with what the Holy Spirit wants for us and what satan wants to take away from us. The Spirit wants us to be free from the binding effects of sin. Satan wants us to be in bondage throughout eternity. We must walk in faith under the Authority of God's Holy Word allowing God to reign over every aspect of our life. This ensures that we will have absolute victory over the sinful desires of our heart.

I was sitting on the couch across from Larry, inhaling the power of illusion from the weed that I was smoking. All of a sudden, because I didn't notice it before, Larry pulls out a long glass tube; the kind that you buy from those little convenient stores with the roses in them. He put fire to one end and inhaled as though he were smoking on a cigarette. I watch for a moment. He held the smoke in his mouth and then he slowly exhaled as the look of total calm appeared on his face as he sat there staring into the ceiling. I now realize why he declined to partake from the plate of my annuals (weed). The competition from the strength and vigor of his cylinder of mysterious cloud vapor overpowered the contents within my hand. What he had to offer was an elevation into the peak of perfection with a sudden decline into the valley of no return. I had never seen anything like it before. He lit and inhaled again. The aroma intrigued me. I said to him, "What are you smoking?" Then I asked him to let me try. He looked at me through the top of his wire framed glasses and said, "You don't want any part of this." He was trying to warn me about a dead end road. If I traveled onto that road my ability to detour would become lost in the night. He was speaking from experience. The road Larry was talking about was a one way road downhill; a road that would not yield and would not bend. It was a road that only gravitated to the bottom.

I suppose a part of Larry wanted to relinquish authority from his cup of despair before the grave called and he could do nothing but answer. But he found himself without the ability to rise and take hold of the reigns. And he surely didn't want to invite me on that journey with him. Yet here I was joining the parade uninvited. I started reciting drama over and over again about having a strong mind and how I could "handle what he had." I told him that I'd been indulging in the haze from smoking marijuana for years and that I've never been hooked, in fact, I told him that I could stop smoking weed at any time and he had no need to worry about my desire to enlist in his hospitality of secrets, for I had everything under control. I just wanted to try what he had one time. Eventually through my persistence Larry gave in. I suppose he really just got tired of me killing his "buzz" because I kept nagging him over and over, I just wouldn't give him any room to breathe.

My life as I knew it, changed forever. A dark veil moved across my face. My body felt as though my soul fell into a deep pit. My hope was gone. My joy had disappeared in an instance. It was as though someone reached in and grabbed everything that made me, me. I dried up on the inside. I had lost the ability to express any true feelings or emotions. I was void of life. On the street that pit is better known as, "That great one." I watched the layers of my life unfold as my soul divorced my body and ascended into the atmosphere. It was the most amazing journey of my entire life and the most destructive. They call it that great one because you will never ever experience such height and devastation at the same time; no matter how many times you try. Instead you spend the rest of your life chasing and falling from the safety and shelter of God's grace. In one moment I created the biggest tragedy of my life. I felt that great one, and then I was hooked. The fall was overwhelming to me. I felt hollow inside.

It was an experience like none other. I had passed beyond the clouds and awakened a dark space within myself. I began to experience true, clear insight through auditory imagination, and illusion. I was tripping. Voices rang clear within my mind, the sound of a great debate. "Stop," the voices rang loud; "do not enter beyond this point." My mind began to fall as through space as the voices echoed in my head. Fear and excitement overcame me and I wanted to reach an even greater height. My heart began to pound. If I continue what will I find? I was afraid of finding the dark side of me. Yet I couldn't stop. I was both embarrassed and ashamed as natural light filled my face and I came back to reality. How long I asked myself had I been experiencing this high. What was Larry thinking as he watched me for the first time take my first hit of crack cocaine? It was unreal. And for me it lasted all but 2 minutes; a small amount of time to pay for what resulted in almost a decade of pain.

I opened my eyes. My head was spinning as memories of childhood merry-go-rounds and people laughing filled my mind. "What have I done?" I asked myself. I entered a race that I could not win. I became paranoid as I peeked through the curtains that hang in the front room of the apartment that overlooked the city. I was sure that I heard a siren. And I was sure that the police were coming to arrest me. I gathered my things and I watched and waited quietly as I listened for a knock on the door. I asked myself, was I going to run, was I going to hide my things? But the police car with its sirens blazing passed me by. They went down the street on their way to some other call. That old saying is true. Don't play around with fire if you don't want to get burnt. I believe that because I heard a police siren the first time I smoked crack cocaine, is the very reason that my paranoia remained in the forefront of my addiction.

I spent years; seven in all trying to achieve that initial feeling. (That great one). Drinking beer could no longer make me feel that high. Smoking weed surely couldn't make me feel that high. But I knew that I had to feel it again. Just once more. No matter how many times I tried, I never felt it again. Not even in the seven years of my addiction. What a waste of time. Instead I became alienated from my family. The only friends that I kept were smokers themselves. No one else understands that world and no one else in their right mind wants to be around people that are in that world; my world became a world of smoking, living in crack houses and arguing over the last blast. They say that "high" insight is worth 20/20. Today my eyes are wide open. My vision is clear. If I only knew then what I know now; believe me I would have never tried crack cocaine. I tried it for fun; but it wasn't fun. Being paranoid just isn't fun. I can't truly describe how I felt, only that my soul was being summoned. My mind was being drawn, and my body craved to "feel," anything. What I felt was paranoia. I found my refrigerator empty, because I would rather get high than buy food. I found out that my furniture was missing and I couldn't call the police because I was the one who stole it to buy more crack.

Larry had warned me not to take that hit, but I pleaded and begged. I just had to try it. I told him that my mind was strong enough to handle it. Even though Larry was a smoker, after I took my first hit, my addiction and craving grew greater than his ever was. Once I became an addict, I wanted to smoke every minute of every day.

To shine light of the devastating situation that I had incurred, as my addiction grew, I want to make it clear...I began neglecting my responsibility as a mother. Eventually, I lost contact with my family, then I lost contact with my money, then I lost contact with myself as I began to neglected my basic needs for survival, and finally I lost contact with my job. I couldn't even find the emotion inside of me to care that I had no place to live. It didn't happen overnight; it happened through time. My addiction started with alcohol; which led me to smoking weed; which led me to smoking crack cocaine, all of which took time.

Crack cocaine however was instantaneously addictive. I didn't wake up one day and say to myself; today I think that I want to become an addict. I didn't wake up one day and say that I'm tired of having a nice job; a place to stay; a car to drive; children to raise; and a family that loves me. I didn't wake up one day and say that I'll give everything up and live outdoors; underneath the under path; living behind garbage dumpsters and eating out of trash cans. I didn't say any of that. What I said was; it's just a one time shot. Why not try it? What harm could it do?

It was as though I was living my life with blinders on. I only wanted to see what was right in front of me. I didn't want to focus on the consequences of my life choices. I told myself everyone has problems. My problem was crack cocaine. It made it much easier for me to drop out of life than to face those problems head on. I developed a serious problem. Me. I became my biggest problem.

Chapter 2

The Ripley's Hook-Up

The Vallejo Elite was the name of my son John's little league baseball team. One summer the team entered a tournament and he needed money for a plane ticket to Kansas City. I took my rent money and bought both of us a ticket. It was quite an experience. When I returned home I had an eviction notice on the front door of the apartment that I was renting on Werden Way. My addiction was intensifying and I hadn't even noticed, but it must have happened enough that The Realty Company felt the need to kick me out. I must have missed rent payments before, I really don't remember. My son had already been staying with my parents on the weekend; but after I lost my apartment, my daughter and my son started staying there permanently. I moved in with Larry. At least the last time that I was late with my rent money was for a good reason. It wasn't about drugs; it was about providing the opportunity for my son to go to Kansas City. I do know that much.

At first staying with Larry was dangerously fun and captivatingly addictive. Even so he and I both still managed to go to work. I had not lost my job yet. Soon I began getting high every day and it manifested itself into my demise. I went downhill quickly casting my sober years out to sea as I became consumed with achieving the state of incapacitation. After about three months into it, Larry didn't want to have anything else to do with me; that's when he asked me to leave. Be that as it may, I'd show up to his house pounding on the door trying to get in. Larry didn't want the neighbors peeking out their windows or opening up their doors (all up in his business), trying to see who was doing the pounding, so eventually he'd let me in. Once I got inside, he could see that all I really wanted to do was to get high. What happened, how did I get to this point in my life? What about my children, what were they doing while I was busy getting high? Did I even keep in contact with them? I can't even answer these questions. I just know that I stayed trapped in my addiction for seven years. Finally Larry had enough of my antics so he told me that I couldn't come back and if I did he would call the police.

Years earlier before I met Larry I was seeing this guy named Bennie, also known as Cheyenne. During this time I was staying with my oldest brother in his house. My brother and other members of my family thought that Bennie was having a negative influence on me. They thought that he was the cause of me smoking weed. The truth of the matter is that I smoked long before Bennie and I got together. It was just that our relationship intensified the addiction. It kind of placed a magnifying glass on the way that I was living my life. So my family was against our relationship. I knew Bennie when I was growing up, he and my second oldest brother were friends. A couple of years after I got out of the Army I ran into him and we started seeing each other. In my mind he was still the same guy that I remembered as a child.

One day I came home, my daughter was about 7 or 8 years old and my son was about 2 or 3 years old, all of our belongings were on the front lawn of my oldest brother's house. He had placed boxes of our things there: my children's clothes, their toys, pots and pans, books, bicycles, everything that we owned was on the front lawn for everyone in the neighborhood to admire. I never had a conversation with my brother and he never mentioned that he wanted us to leave; he just tossed my things outside on the front lawn like rubbish. He didn't like Bennie coming around. It was his house and his decision to kick me and my two children out. I only wish that he could have gone about it differently. Today when I think about that situation I can understand why my brother did what he did. But back then it felt to me as though the rug had been pulled right from under me. My life had bottomed out as I stood there motionless, wondering what I was going to do and where I was going to take my children. I was furious, and for a moment I wanted to take a brick and smash all of the windows to his house. I wanted the windows to shatter and echo the humiliating sound of sorrow. Surprisingly Bennie talked me out of it. The only thing that I could do was leave.

THE RIPLEY'S HOOK-UP

Even in the midst of my tribulation the Lord protected me and provided shelter for me and my children. We were without a place to stay for only one day. Barbara Shane from Vallejo Realty allowed us to move into an apartment. My children never knew that we were homeless. They only remember that we went to the park. I took them there while I was waiting for the paperwork to be completed by the Realty Company. When it was time to move into our new place, I drove to my brother's house, gathered our belongings from the front lawn and we were out of there. I never went inside to ask my brother why he was so cruel in the way he handled the situation. I never said goodbye or anything; we just left. Today everything between my brother and I is just fine. I guess that's what they mean by tough love.

When I moved into my own apartment I allowed Bennie to spend the night every now and then. It wasn't a permanent situation. About two months later we broke up because he stole ten dollars from me and my kids. I asked him to go to the store to buy some milk, he never came back. I went looking for him. I wasn't going to let him get away with that. My children needed their milk and I needed my change. I knocked on a lot of doors, I finally found him at some friend's house. The money was gone. He had spent it on drugs. That's when I found out that Bennie was smoking something other than weed. Up to this point the only bad habits that either one of us had, or I thought we had was smoking weed and drinking beer. In those days I wasn't about to put up with any other drug addictions, especially around my children. Crazy me, not realizing that drugs in any form around our children isn't a good thing. Later that night when he came to the apartment I told him that he couldn't come in, and he had to go. I was finished dealing with Bennie. No one was going to steal from me and my kids.

We argued. Things got out of control and Bennie placed me in a choke hold; somehow during the struggle I managed to get to the kitchen drawer. Inside was a hammer. I grabbed it and tried to hit Bennie with it. He grabbed my arm with his hand and twisted my arm behind my back. As the hammer dropped out of my hand, he picked it up and started hitting me. All I could do was lay down on the floor in the fetal position and cover my head and face with my arms. I kept thinking; if he hits me in the head I'm going to die and the outline of my dead body would remain forever engraved in the black tablets of Hades.

Bennie beat me down with that hammer until I was battered and beaten almost to a pulp. I had a bloody nose, my glasses were broken, and my arms ached. When the fight was over Bennie fled out of the door. When I realized that he was gone I wobbled to the door and I chased after him. Why? I really don't know because I could hardly walk. Sometime during the struggle Bennie hit me in my left knee. I hadn't even noticed that my knee was injured until much later that night after the situation calmed down.

I followed him down the street. I don't know why I didn't just call the police. Maybe it was because the adrenalin was rushing through my veins. I caught up with Bennie about 4 blocks away (by then he had started walking). I think that he thought that he was in the clear. I started hitting him on his shoulders, and anywhere else that I could find with a big stick that I had taken from the yard before I left the apartment.

All of a sudden the police drove up. They could see the bruises on my arms. My arms looked like Popeye's. They were so swollen from me trying to block the blows from Bennie trying to hit me in my face when we were in the apartment. I had red marks on my neck from being in a choke hold. My blouse was torn and I was bleeding from the struggle. The police put both of us in separate police cars and took us to the station. I was in one room and Bennie was in another. I told my side of the story and he told his. We both got sited for mutual combat. I suppose if I didn't try to fight back, Bennie would have been charged with assault and I would have been dead, but because I chased him and fought, we were both charged. The police charge you with the crime of mutual combat when they don't want to deal with the domestic violence situation.

They released me and I went home. The last thing I remember, Bennie was sitting in the police station begging me to change my story. I thought Bennie had gone to jail; after all I was the one that had been brutally beaten. I wasn't able to do much damage to Bennie with the stick because the police came before I really had an opportunity; but about two hours later at 3 o'clock in the morning, I was lying down when he showed up at my door and started pounding his fist on the door. It sounded like thunder as the vibrations echoed through the apartment. I thought he was going to break the door down. I jumped up and crept slowly over to the door. I stood frozen as I placed my ear against the door and listened quietly. I held my breath, afraid to even breathe. My apartment had only one way in and one way out. I was trapped and too afraid to climb out of the window. I couldn't leave without getting into another confrontation with Bennie. I tried to act as if I wasn't home. He yelled out that he had a steal pipe and that he was going to bust my window if I didn't open the door. I took my house shoes off so that I wouldn't make any noise, then I stepped away from the door and walked slowly and quietly to the kitchen drawer and pulled the knob out ever so gently; my heart was pounding in my neck. Bennie yelled out, "I see you." I quickly grabbed a knife being ever so careful not to make a sound, I didn't want him to know what I was trying to do for fear that he would bust the door down. I walked slowly over to the window. I grabbed the cord to the window shade so that I could pull the blinds open, thinking to myself that this man is crazy, what if he has a gun. I was terrified. I opened the blinds slightly and showed him that I had a big knife in my hand and I wasn't kidding. Then I closed the blinds quickly. I told him if he tried to come in, I was going to kill him. I told him that he couldn't get in without passing over the threshold of the door and if he did I was going to stab him in the heart. I believe that if he would have tried to come in, I would have gone through with my threat out of pure fright.

    I can't explain what it feels like to be so terrified when you're whole body is shaking, your knees are trembling and you can hardly breathe. I knew that I couldn't over power Bennie if he somehow came into my apartment, but I knew that I was going to have to do whatever it took to survive. Even if that meant that I had to stab him in the heart with the knife.

I was petrified as I waited at the door, hoping and praying that Bennie would get tired of waiting and leave; just the thought of knowing that I might have to fight this man all by myself caused me to panic. Sweat and fear drenched my blouse as I quivered in the grey shadows of the room. I didn't realize it then, but I wasn't alone.

It's comforting knowing that God says that he will fight our battles; that He would go before us and protect us from the enemy; that there is safety in abiding in the presence of God. Psalms 91 verse 1-6 says: He who dwells in the secret place of the Most High shall abide under the shadow of the Almighty. I will say of the Lord, He is my refuse and my fortress; my God, in Him I will trust. Surely He shall deliver you from the snare of the fowler and from the perilous pestilence. He shall cover you with His feathers, and under His wings you shall take refuge; His truth shall be your shield and buckler. You shall not be afraid of the terror by night, nor of the arrow that flies by day, nor of the pestilence that walks in darkness, nor of the destruction that lays waste at noonday.

The Lord placed a cover of protection over me that night. I didn't have to deal with Bennie. He left and I never saw him again until about six years later. He came through the Arco gas station where I was washing windshields with my boyfriend Big Moosie. Big Moosie chased him away after I told him who Bennie was and what he had done to me. Even now I have problems with my knee. Sometimes the pain is unbearable.

Now here I was again; Larry had pulled the rug right from under me. I was devastated. I had nowhere to go. I had money in my pocket because I had just gotten paid. I was trying to decide if I was going to get a Motel room or something to smoke and just sleep in my car. I drove up and down the streets of Vallejo looking for a place to stay. I found myself, behind the wheel of my car in the middle of the street totally oblivious to my surroundings trying to figure out my next move.

Someone came up to my window and asked me if I wanted to buy some weed. That was the last thing that I wanted right now. I was worlds away from wanting to experience a weed high again. I had graduated to a new and different elevation in life. I wanted to smoke some crack but I didn't know a lot of people in the game, just Larry's folks, but the last time I bought anything from them, they "Rooked me," so I never tried to buy anything from them again.

I can't say that it was perfect timing but I was sure glad to see him at my window.

I can't remember the dealers name and that's okay because this is not a "tell all" about who was the big drug dealer or who sold what to who. It's a story about my life and how I overcame addiction, nevertheless most of the names in this story have been changed to protect those who need protecting. What difference does it make? I wasn't looking for a name, I was looking for a dealer, and he was the one. I gave him Larry's address so that he could meet me in the parking lot. I got my issue of crack and left, but before I left I got his phone number.

Even though I was new to the game, this guy knew how the game worked. If he served me proper in the beginning, he knew that I would want to spend more. Why not bring it to me? That would eliminate the possibility that I might find another dealer. After I smoked my first issue I gave him a call and I waited in the parking lot for him to come so that I could buy more.

For all intended purposes I'll call him Ripley's, because believe it or not, he served me "way more proper" for my little $20 than I had ever been served by Larry. I had the "hook up," he became my connection. And I demanded to be served proper. Once he brought me the stuff he knew that he had a loyal customer. Loyalty in the game is very important. People can get hurt when someone is not loyal.

Relationships are built on Loyalty also; and loyalty is built on trust. My children trusted me to be there for them throughout their entire lives. They trusted me to take care of them and love them unconditionally. They trusted me to be their mother forever and always. My children got hurt because I wasn't loyal to them. I was too busy being loyal to the streets. I hurt my children because I abandoned them. I left them with relatives while I faded away.

Since I had convinced myself that pot was harmless and by smoking it once in a while I couldn't harm anyone, not even the relationship that I had with my children. I soon convinced myself that smoking crack cocaine was harmless as well. How else could I justify abandoning my children.

A day in the life of a crack head last forever. For me I never saw the signs that were leading me down the road of addiction, I just know that one day I wasn't an addict and the next day I was. When I started smoking; an "itty bitty" piece on the pipe went a long way. But now I was hooked and I needed more than ever to achieve the ultimate thrill that left me breathless and wanting more, and Ripley's was just the one I needed for the hook up. At first I spent $20, then I spent $40, later I spent $100. I kept spending until my paycheck was all gone.

I used whatever money I had. I used my rent money, my bill money, even my food money. All that I had, I used. When the money was gone, I used my car as a taxi cab for others seeking to find that same venomous candy coated package of detestable deception.

I never used my body to earn money to get high and I never would. That doesn't make me any better or any worse than someone who felt that they had to do that. That was their business. That's between them and the Lord.

What saved me from that lifestyle was the fortunate fact that I meet Big Moosie (the man that I later married); he showed me a different way to earn money. He showed me the profit to be made in washing windshields at the Arco Gas Station in South Vallejo. I'll tell you how I met Big Moosie later.

In return for a ride in my car to buy dope, I'd get a small portion of the issue. I spent more money in gas than the hit was worth.

I allowed this intruder of deception known as crack cocaine to come into my life, and take complete control over me. It became my "bookie." What I mean by that is; I placed a bet on my own life every day, every hour, every minute. If the truth be told. Every time I got high; it was as though I was making a bet to see if I would live or die.

I found out something quite interesting about the narcotic, rock cocaine; it didn't care about me and it didn't care what I thought. Rock cocaine conned me out of 7 years of my life with empty promises of splendor and poise. Television personality Judge Greg Mathis once said, "Crack Cocaine is a jealous mistress." He's right. Crack cocaine never lets you sleep. It offers no rest for the body and no peace for the "soul." It consumes all of your time as it consumes your entire life.

.

Chapter 3

The Chicken Coop

Something was happening to me. My outlook on life was changing. My appearance had declined. I'd go for days without showering or changing my clothes. I'd stopped caring about going to work. I was so ashamed of the person that I had become and I was embarrassed of what I was doing to myself and how I had allowed this drug to consume me. When I'd get off of work I wouldn't go home, I'd just hang out at the park; anywhere but home. The thought of seeing the disappointed look on my family's face would have been more than I could bear.

I was living a part of life on the street that I had never seen before; at least not in the way that I was seeing it this time, up close and personal; from the view of an addict. My days of weed smoking were long gone; instead my addiction transformed itself and I walked right into the fast lane of my life.

One day I found myself in Hans Park sitting in my car with all of the windows rolled up on a hot summer day, feeling alone and disillusioned popping sleeping pills into my mouth, wearing the same thing that I had on when I came into this world; my Birthday suit.

I could smell the dry heat from the dashboard of my car penetrating my nostrils. My throat quivered as I inhaled and exhaled the pain within my soul. A pain so terrible and so devastating my head felt as if it were about to explode. I held my face in my hand and I cried. Tears streamed from my blood shot eyes and down the sides of my cheeks. As each tear pooled to the end of my face, into my ear, down my neck and splashed onto my shoulder, I felt defeated to the point of exhaustion. I couldn't find the strength within myself to fight.

When Larry threw me out; my addiction overpowered every good and decent feeling within my life; I was wasting all of my money on drugs. I was extremely depressed and I wanted out of this life forever.

I left Vallejo and went somewhere where no one knew me. That day I had gone to Fairfield. I wanted to get high, one last time. I was going to take the ultimate blast of the century and leave this earth forever.

When I close my eyes I can still feel the pain and agony that ruled over my life. I can still feel the sorrow and regret that held me hostage. I was chained in defeat and shackled to a mischievous spirit called darkness. If you have ever been in true darkness; you can't see anything. There is no glimmer of light and no glimmer of hope; only stumbling in the dark.

I found myself in a chicken coop. At least that's what it looked like to me. The walls were made of chicken wire. The floors were covered in dirt. There were feathers and chicken poop everywhere, but it was big enough for a person to stand in. At the time it seemed like the perfect place. It was a cage sure enough, and it seemed fitting to how my life was going. I was a prisoner to my own addiction; caged in my own iniquity.

It really didn't matter where I got high that day; the end result was going to be the same. I felt ashamed and I was so tired. I just wanted my life back, but I didn't know how to get it back. I didn't have the strength to fight the battle within myself. Instead of fighting for my life, I gave up. I went to Fairfield that day to end my life. I bought a "50 pop." and placed the entire thing on the pipe, melted it down and braced myself to take the biggest hit of my life. This would be the first time that I had smoked more than a dime piece at one time. I thought that if I smoked the entire "50 pop" in one wop, my heart would stop beating, my breath would leave my body and my life would end, and all of my troubles would be over.

After I took the blast I started hearing voices like the time when I took my first hit at Larry's house. I lifted my head expecting to see someone, but no one was there. I could hear some type of dialogue being spoken, I sat still and I tried to listen closely, but it wasn't clear. I thought surely it must be my imagination since the voice seemed to be carried by the wind. It was as if the voice was talking about me and the outcome of my life. I tried to speak, but my voice was trembling. I stood up and raised my arms towards the horizon and I called out, "satan if this is a fight you're not going to win. I knew in the back of my mind that satan was behind the voices that I was hearing. For a moment I wondered what if the voices were actually angels warning me of the imminent danger that I was placing myself in. Whether angels or demons, I didn't want satan to get any of the glory. So I stood up and I shouted "you might win this battle, but you will not win the war. Jesus will win in the end! God is more powerful than you. God is and will always be more powerful than you, and the Lord will always be victorious."

Here I was attempting to end my life, yet, somehow I knew that God would intervene before I took my last breath. I wasn't tempting the Lord but I didn't want satan to get any of the glory. Please understand that I had taken the blast already and there was no turning back. Yet I knew that God would show Himself in the end. But I had no idea that the battle would last for seven years. The number seven represents completion. In the book of Joshua 6:1-27, it talks about the battle of Jericho when Israel defeated the city. It is here where the relevance of the number seven is also seen. Each day the people of Israel marched around the city one time, they did this for six days, but on the seventh day, seven priests each held a trumpet and marched around the city seven times. On the seventh day the priests blew the trumpets and the walls of Jericho crumbled to the ground.

The beginning of my seven years started inside of that chicken coop where the angel of the Lord began to march around my life for six years attempting to draw me nearer to Jesus. My pain lasted for a long time. In the seventh year I finally listened.

There inside of that chicken coop; I had been hallucinating? I was confused. Was I insane? Whether I was or not; I couldn't stop myself from going through with my plan to kill myself.

After I smoked that entire "50 pop," my life didn't end. I was still alive and still deeply depressed. I was determined more than ever to finish what I had started. I still wanted my life to end. Because this drug called crack cocaine distorts your mind. The voices that I heard had me thinking that I must be insane. So I gathered my things and returned to Vallejo.

On the drive home I convinced myself once again that I truly must be insane. I told myself that I was going to end up like one of those crazy people talking to themselves on the street. I didn't want to end up like that and I didn't want my family to see me like that.

As the drug was wearing off, I told myself that God couldn't possibly care about a "nobody" like me. If God didn't care about me, why should I care? It was easier to say that God didn't care about me than to say that I didn't care about myself. How else could I justify my decision to end my life?

I began to wallow in self-pity. That's a dark and dirty place to be. Self-pity will not allow faith to grow. You see faith is always there waiting on us to water it. But because of the self-hatred that I was feeling; the thorns of my problems chocked out faith and would not allow it to grow. I was blaming God for my situation. As if God had placed that crack pipe to my mouth. I asked myself why God was allowing this to happen to me. Not realizing that I was the cause of my own self-hatred. I'm not saying that my problems were anywhere near the type of problems that Job in the Bible had when he went through his loss. But I can understand how devastated he must have felt as his life seemed to move so far away from God's mercy and grace, when he said in Job 10:18-22, "Why then did you bring me out of the womb? I wish I had never come into being, or had been carried straight from the womb to the grave! Are not my few days almost over? Turn away from me so I can have a moment's joy before I go to the place of no return, to the land of gloom and deep shadow, to the land of deepest night, or deep shadow and disorder, where even the light is like darkness."

It was time for me to make the necessary final arrangements to end my life. I went to the ATM and got $60 out of an account. Then I went to Safeway and purchased a bottle of sleeping pills. Then I went to 7-11 and bought a 40 ounce bottle of beer. I went down the street and got another $50 pop. I went to different stores so that no one would suspect me of trying to overdose. Then I went to a nearby payphone and made a call to my employer at the Maritime Academy. It was the weekend and I knew that no one would be in the office to answer the phone. I wanted to leave some type of message for my family. I was afraid to call home. I couldn't face the thought of hearing my family's voice on the other end of the phone as I told them what I was going to do. With tears rolling down my face, I cried hysterically into the phone. The message I left said that I was going to end my life and that I was sorry for being such a disappointment.

My intention was to consume the entire bottle of sleeping pills, drink the 40 ounce bottle of beer and smoke the 50 pop. I forgot one crucial part of the plan, I have difficulty swallowing pills. I had to place each pill one by one in my mouth as I held my tongue down with my fingers. Each time, I consciously made the decision to continue with my plan. I popped a pill to the back of my throat. After each pill, I took a big swig of beer until I had nearly taken all but one sleeping pill; I wanted to save the last pill for the finale. As I stated earlier I got this idea in my head that I would leave this world the same way that I came in. So I got out of the car and peeled off my clothes and got into my Birthday suit, then I got behind the wheel of my car.

As I waited for the sleeping pills to take effect, I began worrying fanatically about the problems in my life and how easy I was finding it to give up hope. Little did I realize I was about to cheat myself out of a blessing. My life didn't belong to me, it belongs to the Lord. I was bought with a price. Jesus took upon Himself the sins of the world. That meant that He knew what I was going through. He knew all about my situation and the sorrow that I was feeling so deep inside of myself. He was beaten for our iniquities; By His stripes (His wounds) we are healed. Surely I could bear my pain for a little while longer. If I could; then I would find out what it feels like to be healed. But I was a coward. I gave up.

Yes we are going to have trials and tribulations in this world. It's inevitable. But we don't have to bear them alone. God sent us a comforter; someone who will put into words the groaning that we feel so deep within our spirit; someone who can feel the pain that is felt to the core of our existence and brings them before the Father for understanding and deliverance. That someone is the Holy Spirit. Therefore remember that no matter what we are going through, God is able to deliver us from our circumstances. God just wants a chance to use each and every one of us if we'd only give Him a chance. Stand still and behold the power of The Almighty God; The Alpha and the Omega; The Beginning and the End. He wants us to know that we can depend on Him. Just call on the name of His Son Jesus; The One who stands in the gap; who petitions the Father in our behalf for our behalf. The Name of Jesus, He is more than a conqueror. Step out on faith and yield to His Words.

This Battle is not ours, it belongs to the Lord. He feels all of our pains, and knows everything that we are going through. Everything is going to work out according to His Perfect Plan, and His Holy Will. My story has a lot of pain, a lot of sadness, and a lot of grief. It even has joy and laughter. But hold on for one moment and allow me to continue to share with you my struggle that you may know that God is real.

You see I've been through the battle; I've been through the storm. And with the Lord's help, I came out on the other side victorious. You too can be victorious. Whatever the situation, God can fix it. I've been to Hell and back. I want to take the opportunity to stop you in your tracks so that you don't have to go down that same dark and lonely road that I did.

As I was saying; on that dark day, after I had taken about 39 sleeping pills I began to cry. I thought about my life and how messed up it was because of what I was doing. I told myself I was worthless and that my life was not worth living. I told myself that I was going to die in my car. My car was going to become my coffin. I thought about how hurt my family would be when they found me, but I also felt that they would be better off without me. I took a deep breath and I blew the air from my lungs causing my body to calm. I can't explain this calm only that it was like a strong tide rushing in and out. You can hear the pounding of the tide as it beat against the rocks; yet with each rushing wave the gentle sound and rhythm echoed silence and serenity. I had cried all of the tears that I could cry. Then I took the 40th pill, the last pill; the pill that symbolized the end of my existence. I sat in the driver's seat with my head held back sobbing and knowing that my time would soon run out. Darkness was upon me and my life would soon be over.

Suddenly I heard a tap on the rear passenger window of my car. Someone in the neighborhood had called the police after seeing me standing outside in my Birthday suit. They must have thought that I was exposing myself in the park but I was really getting ready to die. The paramedics came; they motioned for me to roll down my window. Couldn't they understand that all I needed was a few minutes more and my life would be over? I wasn't about to open the door or roll down the window. I wouldn't cooperate.

Suddenly I heard "Thug." My back right passenger window had been shattered. The paramedics had taken a big object and broke the glass. They reached inside and opened the door. A police officer came around to the driver's side where I was sitting behind the wheel. By that time all of the other car doors were open. The officer started asking me all sorts of questions as he pulled me out of the car. He wanted to know what I was doing in the park. At first I wouldn't tell him anything. I didn't care. In my mind I felt it was already too late for anyone to do something about my situation anyway. I had already taken my last hit, drank my last beer and taken my last sleeping pill and I was just waiting for my last breath. I was just waiting for my life to end. Couldn't they see that I just wanted to be left alone?

The police gathered my personal information from my wallet and presented it to the dispatcher; she informed them of my hysterical phone call to my job earlier in the day stating that I wanted to end my life. My job had already called my family to find out what was going on with me. And someone had called the police. Everyone was already looking for me. I can't imagine what my family must have been going through when they heard of my plans. They must have been going out of their minds. I hadn't thought about that. I only knew that everyone would be better off without me.

After the officer reached inside of my car to grab me; the paramedics set me down and began taking my vital signs. I felt like I was walking in a fog. Every step that I took was as though my limbs didn't belong to me. It was as though I was disconnected from my body. I didn't feel hurt and I didn't feel pain. I wasn't sad and I wasn't mad. In fact I felt nothing at all. My entire body was numb. I laid my head calmly back in surrender and agreed to let the paramedics take me to Kaiser Hospital. I was rushed to the Emergency Room. They connected me to a monitor and all of the usual hook ups. Someone asked me what I had taken. I don't remember if I gave them an answer or not but the nurse stated that if they couldn't determine what I had taken then they would have to pump my stomach. I wouldn't tell them anything. I was buying time, in hopes that my plan would still work.

Immediately a tube was placed down my throat. I didn't expect that. Then I was given charcoal which caused the contents of my stomach to come out. I was fading in and out. The next thing that I remember was being inside of an ambulance and the EMT saying to me that they were transporting me to another facility, the psychiatric hospital on Broadway.

My attempted suicide was a cry for help. I know that now. I could have gone to jail that night, because I did have drug paraphernalia in the car; but the officer calmly talked me into cooperating and going to the hospital instead. I spent about thirty days in the psychiatric hospital. On my first night, there was a plate of food on the night stand next to my bed. I looked at it off and on for a long time. I decided not to eat so I left it there. Later the psychiatrist nurse came by. She asked me if I knew why I was there. Everything seemed surreal. I couldn't really remember. The only thing that I could remember was getting into the ambulance. She asked me if I wanted to die. I didn't have an answer for her.

I do remember that as I lay in bed that night, I felt different. The person that I remembered in my youth no longer existed. I was so sad. I couldn't even face myself and I surely couldn't face my family. My father and my sister came to visit one time; I think it was too hard for anyone else. I told the doctors that I didn't want any more visits. I only allowed them to visit me then because they had already come and I didn't want to turn them away. The truth is I hadn't decided what I wanted to do. Just because I survived didn't mean that I wanted to survive.

Later that night I kept looking at the plate of food on the night stand next to my bed. I was trying to decide if I was going to eat or just let them take it away again. Did I want to live or did I really want to die? I decided to eat, by eating; it proved that I really didn't want to die.

I guess I finally had the answer for the psychiatrist nurse. A person can't want to die and eat to sustain life at the same time. The sad thing about it was that something could have gone wrong and I could have died anyway. That's what I meant when I said that I could have missed out on my blessing; because my life is just beginning. I've found my purpose in life. Writing this book is one way that I have of giving back what the devil tried to steal from me. If it hadn't been for someone calling the police because of my strange behavior in the neighborhood, I just might have gotten my wish to die. Then I would have really been lost. I would have been dead, never knowing the true love and forgiveness of God. If you ever feel as though your life is out of control, or you feel that no one cares about you, or you are simply looking for a good time. Take it from me. You won't find it on the end of a crack pipe.

But I can tell you this. You can find everything that you need when you call upon the name of Jesus. Jesus represents deliverance, power, truth and grace. Everything that is good. Remember Jesus cares about you. God only wants the very best for us. Many people endure pain in life, at the end of that pain, most often they can find the good that came out of it. I said things that I later regretted. Things like God didn't care about me. I should have remained loyal to God, not for what He has done for me, but simply for who He is.

When I made up my mind to surrender my addiction to the Lord; with the help of the Holy Spirit; I was able to climb up out of the pit that I had placed myself in. It was a long haul but I finally got there. Allow me to share the rest of my journey with you. My hope is that by putting my thoughts on paper; I might be able to help someone climb out of their pit. Let me help you climb out of your pit?

Chapter 4

On A Mission

When my thirty days at the psychiatric hospital was up, I entered into the Kaiser Drug and Alcohol Outpatient Treatment Program through my job with the Maritime Academy. The program consisted of group settings with therapists and counselors to help and advise us. Each one was involved in listening to our story. We also had random drug test. Because I had just gotten out of the hospital; I passed my drug test easy. With no drugs in my system, I was feeling pretty good about myself. The program seemed to be working for me. After I had been in the Kaiser program for about a month or so, one of the counselors scheduled a one on one meeting with me. This is where the long haul begins.

One of the most difficult things about my personality is that from the outside most people seem to view me as being a strong minded person who knows what they want and can pretty much cope in certain situations. But what most people don't realize is that it's just a wall that I have in front of me so that in general people aren't able to see my weaknesses. The wall is my protection and there are not many whom I allow to penetrate this wall.

The counselor thought that she understood me and had a fairly good idea about what was going on with me. In her mind she thought that I was ready to take the next step in my recovery. From a few sessions she thought that she was able to break down my wall. During the meeting, I was informed that as part of the "Outpatient Program" I had to join what is commonly known as the "Twelve Step Program." In order to graduate from the outpatient program, I had to complete all twelve steps. I wasn't ready for any of that.

Why did the counselors have to put so much emphasizes on graduating. It's just a title. A day at a time they always said. What was the big rush about graduating? I needed more time in the outpatient program. More time to realize that it wasn't the program that I needed to work for me, but I needed God to work in my life.

Later I found out why the 12 Step Program didn't work for me. God had other plans for my recovery. My recovery was coming from Him and not from man. My recovery would be spiritually based and not based on the world's perception of recovery.

The outpatient program was during the day. The twelve step program was at night. Don't get me wrong; the Twelve Step Program has helped a lot of individuals. But for me; night was my worst time. During the Outpatient Program I stayed at my parent's home. My fear was having the freedom that comes with the night. I had programmed myself to go to the counseling sessions and then go home, eat, watch television, go to bed, and get ready to do the whole thing all over again. I knew that I didn't want or need to be out at night; mostly because I was afraid of what I might do. I felt safe just going home; I didn't have to face life after dark. To face life meant that I had to make decisions for myself. I think that I had proven that I was incapable of making sound decisions right now. I needed time to be on my side.

Just as I had predicted, after each 12 step meeting I just wanted to hang out and get involved in doing wrong things. The 12 step program wasn't helping me with my addition. It was giving me an alibi to hang out.

As the days and nights passed, I began to slip back into my old pattern of behavior. After each 12 step program I started drinking a little beer. I found out that beer is my trigger, a Gateway to other harmful drugs. Beer wasn't enough. Eventually I left one of the meetings and I went to get high. It was inevitable. Once I gave into my trigger it was only a matter of time before I took things to the next level.

At the 12 Step Program I would listen to other addict's vivid expressions about their experiences and how they felt when they got high, that only made me want to do the same thing. So one night I left the 12 Step Program and I went to get high. That night after I got high, I went home, but the damage was done. I couldn't wait until morning. I was on what is called "A mission." If you have been on a mission before then no explanation is necessary. But if you have never been on a mission, then let me explain it to you from my perspective. I was doing really good staying away from drugs, but one night I gave into the temptation after drinking a beer when I left the meeting of the 12 Step Program.

As I mentioned, beer was my gateway into smoking harmful drugs. For me it was smoking crack cocaine again, because drinking beer didn't give me the high that I needed. The sad thing about it was that when I decided to take a hit of crack cocaine, I couldn't just take one hit and leave it alone. So I made it my mission to get some more. So I left my parent's home and went on a mission to get a hit. I had my car still so I thought that maybe I could use it as a taxi cab like I did before. What I found out was that one hit of crack cocaine always leads to wanting more, and the craving is never satisfied, and my seven year mission began.

The next day I told my mother that I was going to wash my car. My family didn't hear from me for six months. When I returned home, I stayed for about a week, and then I was gone again for 7 years. My long haul to redemption continued.

My family looked everywhere for me. I never told them that I was leaving. After everything that I had put them through with my attempted suicide, it was really selfish of me to leave without saying anything. My family heard through the grape vine that I was staying at a crack house. It took my family about six months to find that out. I can imagine how difficult it must have been for them, not knowing if I were dead or alive. Before my attempted suicide, I don't think that my family had a clue that I was using drugs. They might have suspected that I was smoking a little weed from my days with Bennie, but I'm sure they had no idea of the depth of my addiction. Even if they did, they probably didn't know how to confront me. I was the first in my family to go through something like this.

Years later, after I slipped back into my path of destruction; I found out that I didn't need a 12 step program. The Program couldn't help me with my addiction; it had no power to put my addiction to death. God had other plans for me. I only needed one step. Jesus. I just needed to believe in my heart that through Christ I would get well. I only needed to confess with my mouth that Jesus was in charge and surrender all to Him. At the end of my 7 years I found out that I could trust the Lord with all of my heart and my inner thoughts. Through Jesus Christ I could finally be free from the indwelling sin in my life, and be empowered by the Holy Spirit to live for Christ. Through Jesus Christ there is no condemnation to those who set their minds on the things of God. I could be forgiven, and no one could take it away. When the Son of God sets you free you're free indeed. But as it turned out my freedom from sin wouldn't come to reality until much later.

Chapter 5

Big Moosie

After I decided never to go back to the Kaiser's Outpatient Program, when I left my mom's house, and I told her that I was going to go wash my car, I drove to South Vallejo thinking that I could find someone promoting street pharmaceuticals. I was on a mission to find crack cocaine after I relapsed. I saw Tracy standing on the corner. I knew that she would know where to get some dope.

I hadn't seen Tracy since Redtop Road. She was the lady I met when Larry had thrown me out. She let me stay in the back bedroom of her apartment. I stayed at her place about a week. My time there was short lived because when I came home from work one day, I noticed that a lot of my things were missing from the boxes I had in the bedroom. When I confronted Tracy about it, she denied it. I couldn't prove anything so I let it go for the moment. I had a plan in mind. I decided to ask her to take a ride with me to get some dope. She thought I was an easy target because I didn't argue when my things went missing so she thought that she would be able to talk me out of my dope just as easy as she talked me out of believing that she hadn't stolen the things out of my boxes. She thought she "hit a lick" or in other words an easy target.

We got into my car, and headed towards Redtop Road. I took the side road. I pulled over and parked under the highway underpass. When I turned my headlights off, everything was dark. There wasn't even light from the streetlights. I could hear the sound of a rushing wind as the cars drove down the freeway across the overpass. I grabbed my keys from the ignition and I got out of the car. Then I told Tracy to get out. At first she was hesitant; she thought that I was going to leave her stranded out there in the middle of nowhere. All I wanted was the truth from her. I asked about my property. I had lost so much by this point, I wasn't about to let her steal from me. All that I owned fit into those four boxes. I told her if I didn't get my things I was going to kick the crap out of her, then we were going to take a blast and go home. She said that I was crazy.

My plan was to chock her out. I was going to make an example out of her. I was going to beat her down. I knew that I was out there on my own and I didn't want people thinking that I was an easy target. Something on the inside of me kept me from hurting her. We didn't fight. But she never messed me over again. The next morning I moved out.

As it turned out she would be the one responsible for introducing me to Big Moosie who later became my husband. Big Moosie was so charming and pleasant. He had a way about him that set me at ease. I became so relaxed with him by the time I realized it I had already been there about six months. Big Moosie was showing me how the game really worked; and I got caught up.

When I first met Big Moosie, he was sitting at a desk in a room void of any furnishings, except a couch, a table and a chair. He was a man of dark complexion with a smile that warmed the room. He invited me in. I was nervous at first and he could tell. He offered me a seat. I accepted and sat down as the cushions sank to the bottom from the old and torn couch with missing springs. He introduced himself in this deep un-concerning voice as "Big Moosie." We talked for a long while as I reclined into the night. Time seemed to pass by fast. For the first time in the game I actually felt safe enough to relax and enjoy myself. This was a whole new world for me. I didn't want to leave so I stayed. I wasn't ready to go home and I never did. Big Moosie didn't let anyone in the house take advantage of me either, we just partied.

I started smoking more and missing work more. One day I had a talk with Mr. Lee, my supervisor at the Maritime Academy and told him all about my problems and that I wanted to get help. I convinced myself and him that maybe I really wanted the help. But I must admit a part of me knew that I would never go back. I just couldn't face my co-workers and my supervisor knowing about my attempted suicide. I just wanted to establish job security in case I ever got well enough to return to work. My supervisor advised me to seek counseling for my drug addiction. He said after I got the help I needed then we could talk. For the record I took a leave of absence without pay for 1 year. They held my job for 2 years. As predicted I never went back.

In the beginning of our relationship I would go to the Arco Gas Station and watch Big Moosie make his money. In addition, he got a paycheck on the 1st and the 15th of each month from SSI and SSA, in between those times he earned his money washing windshields. Some days he'd be out there for hours and I would just sit in the car and wait.

One day while washing windshields, Big Moosie was having a hard time making money. He came over to where I was sitting and asked me if I could help him wash a couple of windshields. Absolute terror and surprise was on my face as I looked at him. For a moment I thought that surely he must be joking. I thought to myself, I'm not about to get out there and ask people to wash windshields for money. But there was something in the sound of his voice that let me know that he was serious. At first I was petrified. It's not easy to ask a total stranger for money. Moosie started out getting the customers for me, and I would wash the windshields. After a while I got the courage to ask my first customer if I could wash their windshield. Eventually I became pretty good at it and I started earning good money. And that's how we started washing windshields together.

By the time I met Moosie, he had been in the game for a "minute." I'm kind of lucky that I ended up with him. I could have met someone who wanted to "turn me out," instead I met Moosie. He was a Five Star Double O.G. He washed windshields to earn his money. And his girl (me) was going to earn money the same way.

Big Moosie grew up in a Christian Home just like I did. Both of our families taught us the value of working hard and earning money honestly. Both of us lost everything because of our addiction to crack cocaine.

Years before I met Moosie, he had been involved in a car accident. He was an innocent passenger in an open convertible during a high speed police chase. As the car turned the corner the driver lost control of the car. The convertible rolled over and over and over again. Moosie said that his head was dangling out of the car as it skidded down the street. His head banged against everything that wasn't nailed down before coming to a complete stop. He was immediately rushed to the emergency room where they performed major surgery on him. He had a neck injury, but he lived.

The doctors put a metal plate in his head. It's amazing that he was able to walk. Moosie was placed on serious pain medication. Because of his injuries he could no longer work in construction or the oil refinery so he began receiving SSI and SSA. Moosie had become dependent on prescription pain medication, at least in the beginning. When he could no longer get the relief he needed from his doctor, he began using his SSI and SSA to buy street drugs. They provided him with the pain relief that he needed. Then he became addicted. No one who is truly addicted to drugs is happy in that situation. We all want to be a functional part of society. We all want a good education; a great job; a home; and a family that loves us. These things are essential to survival. We all need to eat. We need shelter; and no one wants to be alone.

The house where I first met Moosie got raided and we had to move out. Moosie's friend Sharon, who stayed on the other side of town, let us rent a room in her house. "Traffic" in the house was outrageous. People were coming and going, smoking and drinking, all day long. I hated it there. There were too many people for me. But at the time we had nowhere else to go. The house we were staying in got raided and the police definitely knew what type of activity was going on inside. I wasn't going back. Not even for a visit. We knew that it was just a matter of time before that house would be raided again. How could we relax and enjoy ourselves if at any moment we felt that the police would be back. So I stayed at Sharon's. Wherever Moosie stayed, I stayed.

I knew that smoking made me paranoid. We all had strange ways and that was mine. But just like anyone else in the game, we all shared common ground; we all had relationship problems. The only difference was that ours was compounded and magnified by our daily drug use. That's why I didn't want people watching me. People act different when they get high, especially with a drug like crack cocaine, so I mostly smoked alone.

It might sound funny, but I met some nice people in the crack house. But I knew not to leave my valuables unattended. Crack cocaine will have you stealing from your loved ones just so that you can cop again. It consumes you and robs you of your personality as it destroys your soul. Because crack made me so paranoid I was suspicious of everyone in the house. Once right before taking a really big hit, Moosie and a couple of his friends planted this idea in my mind about this female who had been smoking with us all day. They said that she was an undercover cop and that she was there to bust all of us. Being busted for drug use, now you know that was one of my biggest fears, and Moosie knew it.

After I took a hit, I heard a police siren in my head again; just like I did when I was at Larry's house. I started looking all around the room. The look on my face must have been priceless. I stood up, walked over to where she was and began "Chicken Choking" her. I accused her of being the police. I placed my hands around her neck and lifted her straight up in the air and walked her into the corner of the room with my bare hands. I looked her straight in the eyes with my lips curled trying to look intimidating and demanded that she tell me who she really was. She never confessed. In my head she was the police. In real life I can't tell you who she was. After I came down from my high I realized that I could be wrong. I think I was set up. After that, I wasn't sure if I could trust Moosie anymore. She might not have been the police, but she was somebody that Moosie knew because he brought her there and he used her against me.

Instead of being on my side he ganged up on me. He used my paranoia to entertain his friends. I admit, they got their laughs, but it cost Moosie the trust that I had for him; something that he would have to earn back. His little stunt left me feeling lost and abandoned. It was as though the air that I needed to breath had been shut off and smothered with humiliation and despair. I started questioning our relationship together. If I couldn't trust him with something so sensitive as my paranoia, then I needed to take a closer look at everything else in our relationship. What else couldn't I trust him with? For the first time I thought Moosie was seeing other women. I thought for a moment that he brought that girl to the house just to create a confrontation between us so he could see how we would act towards each other in that situation.

Anyway I insisted that Moosie take that female home or wherever he picked her up. You better believe it, I went with them. I really wanted to see where she lived. It was something about that whole situation that made me hesitant.

Moosie and I began to argue every day after that. When the dope was gone the arguing was on. This put a strain on our relationship. I kept thinking that he was making fun of me behind my back. And that intensified my suspicion. It brought it to the hundredth power of paranoia.

When we weren't smoking crack cocaine, we got along great together. But after that whole scenario we started arguing from the time we woke up until the time we went to bed. The only time we didn't argue was when we were washing windshields. I accused him of cheating; he accused me of entertaining other guys in the house. I might have let the whole situation go if it had not been for the fact that he brought that girl to the house. I was so tire of the bull, I moved out of the bedroom.

I had to get away from Moosie. I pitched a tent in the middle of the living room. How crazy was that? But I did it. Can you imagine putting a tent in the middle of the living room of a house? Not like when you're just playing around with your kids and you make believe that you're camping inside. I actually camped inside of the house. I did that because I didn't trust Moosie anymore, especially since he started acting so jealous. It made him look guilty. When a man keeps accusing his woman of cheating, he's probably the one doing the cheating. Even when we were lying right next to each other in bed Moosie started accusing me of cheating on him and having another man in the bed with me while we were lying together. How could I have a man in bed with Moosie there and he'd not know about it? I guess he thought I must have hid him under the bed or something because he'd look there. And that was Big Moosie's strange behavior when he got high.

The truth of the matter is that I never cheated on Moosie, but I think something happened with him and that girl. When I smoked he couldn't even get any. Why would I have sex with someone else right in front of him anyway? What type of person did he think I was? I loved Moosie.

I lost interest in having sex while high on crack. My high was all about paranoia and making sure that everything around me was clean in case the police came. And just in case the camera crew was with them to report "a breaking news story," What would my family say if they saw me on television getting arrested? Anyway I was tired of it. That's why I moved out of the bedroom. My great idea was short lived anyway since our agreement was to rent one of the bedrooms and not the living room. Sharon told me that I had to move back into the bedroom.

I stayed in that relationship with him because things were fantastic when we weren't smoking. That's when we acted like normal people. That's when I felt safe. No matter how safe and secure we feel even if we have all of the necessities of life; we will always feel incomplete if we don't have a true relationship with the Lord. If we look at the trials and tribulations that we go through in life, instead of complaining about them, we ought to see them as an opportunity to grow. The only way that we can know the depth of our character is to apply pressure and see how we react to it. James 1:2-4 says, "Consider it pure joy, my brothers, whenever you face trials of many kinds, because you know that the testing of your faith develops perseverance. Perseverance must finish its work so that you may be mature and complete, not lacking anything." I'm not saying that we should become fearful when faced with troubles, but rather we should realize that our troubles provide an opportunity to learn; no matter what type of situations we're in or what our circumstances are.

I can't change the fact that I used drugs, I wish that I could. And I can't change the fact that I was the cause of my own trials and tribulations, but I can share with you what drugs took from me. Most of all I can share with you the power of God. He delivered me from the bondage that I put myself in by the poor choices that I made in life.

Hebrews 4:12-13 say, "For the Word of God is living and active. Sharper than any double-edged sword, it penetrates even to dividing soul and spirit, joints and marrow; it judges the thoughts and attitudes of the heart. Nothing in all creation is hidden from God's sight. Everything is uncovered and laid bare before the eyes of Him to whom we must give account."

My account was overdrawn. It would take years before there would be any attempts at making any deposits towards mending my relationship with God and my family by rebuilding my life through faith.

Some people become addicted to alcohol. I became addicted to crack cocaine. After one hit I was hooked. Crack cocaine is no joke. If you are not careful it will snatch you up and throw you away.

Sometimes I think about when my children were younger. I remember watching them play in the park; teaching them to ride their bikes; reading stories to them; sitting on the porch drinking hot chocolate and looking at the stars trying to find the "Big Dipper," or just remembering how precious they were and wishing that I could go back to that time and place. But I can't. Those moments are gone forever.

When I see my children struggling; I know that things could have been different if I'd stayed in their lives. I blame myself for their emotional and financial problems. Don't get me wrong they turned out great. My daughter works in the Dental field and my son went to the Army. They both succeeded in life without me. But things could have been better. Things should have been better.

We're back to being a family now with problems like anyone else. But often I hit myself upside the head because of what I did; most of all because I missed out on so much of their life. I tell myself that I somehow don't deserve to remember those tender sweet moments of innocence that I once shared with my children when they were young. It's as though I tell myself that I don't have the right to remember the part of their childhood that belonged to me when I was a good mother. I had so many hopes and dreams of the way my life should've been when I became a mother for the first time. But I lost my ability to think and make sound decisions as a mother because of my addiction. My motherhood skills were gone. I know that I will be criticized for my life choices, but it was something that happened during my addiction; this drug is that powerful? It's not an excuse; it's just how it was. Crack cocaine dominated my life.

I can't imagine growing up without my mom or my dad. Unfortunately and regretfully my children can remember growing up without me. That's a part of my life that really hurts. My mother says that I lost my mind. She's right. Maybe that's why crack heads walk down the street looking on the ground. Maybe they're looking for the mind that they lost. LOL.

Chapter 6

The Ride

I had just walked in the door of Sharon's house; I hadn't even had a chance to take a blast because I had been working at the Arco all day, when I saw a man of Caucasian decent; wearing a white button-up collar with khaki pants. He was standing in the hallway of Sharon's house listening to everyone's conversations and asking a whole lot of nonsense questions.

He was being overly friendly towards everyone in the house. He seemed a bit nervous to me. He seemed out of place. Like a fish out of water. I walked over to him and asked him his name. He told me something like Mark. I said, "What's up Mark?" He said he was waiting for someone, a friend or something like that. I noticed he kept watching everyone's movements in the house, like he was taking mental notes for a test. He didn't belong there. I wanted to investigate the situation a bit more, so I offered him a hit of crack; I wanted to see if he would take the hit. He wouldn't even take it. I never saw someone come to a crack house and not want a hit. A real crack head would have taken the hit and stayed for more like it was a party just for them. They wouldn't have turned it down for anything in the world. A crack head in a crack house not wanting to take a hit seemed real suspicious to me. If he didn't want to smoke it there, he could have taken it with him. If he wasn't a smoker why was he there? He sure wasn't a dealer. So I watched him as he watched everyone else.

Every time someone asked him his name; he told them something different. So I began to really listen to the conversations that he was having with other people in the house. Finally I walked up to him and told him that I noticed that his name kept changing. I told him that it was mighty strange. He denied it and tried to give me some kind of lame excuse like I must have heard him wrong. I know I couldn't have heard him wrong. I mean how many different interpretations of the name Mark are there. I mean, maybe he said his name was something like Shark. Well Mark and Shark sound alike. Or maybe he said his name was Nark. That sounds more like it since this was a crack house. I thought to myself, "He's the police." I was sure of it. This time I wasn't tripping. Remember I had just walked into the house.

Sharon was in her room so I knocked on the door. When I came in I told her what I thought, but she chalked it up to me being paranoid as usual. She was so used to seeing me like that especially around new people; she thought that I was high from smoking crack. While it's true I was there to smoke; I hadn't had time to do that yet.

I can't blame her, most of the time I was paranoid, but I wasn't paranoid this time, no not this time. I had never seen this so called Mark in the house before. There were so many people living there already, but on this day there were even more people in the house than usual. I had every reason to be suspicious. A set up was getting ready to go down, I just knew it, but no one would listen to me. So I started checking out my surrounding and everything that was going on in the house and I decided that it was time for me to get ghost.

It had me thinking about what I was doing with my life and why I was even living in a crack house and subjecting myself to all of this drama. Finally I had made up my mind to leave Moosie and get away from the situation that was getting ready to go down, so I spent most of the day cleaning my room and packing my things. I only had a few things but they were still my things.

About 4 hours later I really needed a hit, it was time because I hadn't had one all day. Since I already thought that Mark was the police, there was no way that I was going to let him see me take a hit. I didn't care if he thought that I was taking a hit, but I wasn't about to let him see me take it. When a crack head really needs a hit, they're going to find a place to take it. So I went into the bedroom closet as if the closet could protect me. I sat down and closed the door. After I took a hit, I got the courage. I walked out of that closet focused on one thing; I went straight up to Moosie and told him that I made up my mind. It was time for me to leave. I was finally ready to get back to my family. When I was high, the guilt inside of me wanted to do the right thing. The rush that I got when I was high felt like it would last forever. Inside of my twisted thoughts I really felt as though I could leave the dope alone just like that and go back home. In reality, my high didn't last that long. So I had to get another hit. There went another broken promise.

It was getting late and I was almost finished cleaning; I didn't want to give Sharon any reason to charge me for any damages to her place. It sounds crazy but I didn't want to burn any more bridges, with the bad luck that we were having with places to stay I thought that if I cleaned everything up it wouldn't hurt our chances if we needed a place to stay at some other point in time. So I spent most of the day on my hands and knees trying to clean the stains out of the carpet before I moved out.

Earlier that day I told Moosie that I was thinking about leaving, I thought he should know, he said he didn't know what he would do without me. Frankly I didn't know what I would do without him. I didn't want to hurt his feelings, but I needed to do something else with my life. We cared about each other but this whole situation was getting ridiculous. We spent our days and nights either getting high or trying to get high and I couldn't keep on living like that.

I didn't want to just walk away. We had gone through too much together already. I told him that I needed to go home to my family. I told him that my daughter had come by and that I wanted to go back home with her and be with my family.

Every time I started towards the front door with my personal belongings, Moosie followed me. He didn't want me to leave. He kept pleading with me to stay. I understood that. But in my head I desperately needed to leave and get out of that environment.

In the back of my mind I knew that all it would take was one hit of crack cocaine and days and weeks would pass before I realized that I hadn't done anything about leaving. Moosie knew it too, so he made sure that I had enough dope to keep me occupied. He also left me alone because he also knew if he started accusing me of seeing another guy then I would definitely leave.

One way to keep me from leaving was to tell me that his "folks" were coming by with a "fat" package (more drugs). It was working too. It was as though the drug was keeping me hostage. I was in a cage without any bars. I wanted to leave, but I wanted to stay, at least until his "folks" came. We all knew how that would turn out.

My addiction consisted of months passing between the time that I told myself that I wanted to do something constructive like go home to my family and finally go back to work. I knew that before any of that could happen I would need to go back to the program. Each time I tried to leave I would take a hit and I had to stay. I was still determined to get "That Great One," before I got out of the game. I told myself that maybe because I was leaving, I could just take a fat blast and go home. Deep down I knew that the only place that I would go would be back to the Arco to wash some more windshields so that I could make some money for another hit because I would be chasing the hit again. Then I would come down from the hit because I ran out of dope; and I'd tell myself that I wanted to do something constructive. The cycle kept repeating itself. I just couldn't make the change. It was so hard.

But Mark was giving me all the incentive I needed to leave. He was there to bust everybody and I knew it. So I gathered my belongings. When no one was paying any attention to me, especially Moosie, I closed the bedroom door and quietly crawled out of the window. I went down the back alley. My car was parked at the bottom of the hill. It wasn't running at the time, so I crawled in it for the night. I had planned on calling my family in the morning. I really didn't think that Moosie would look for me in the car since it wasn't running. At least that's what I was hoping. I wasn't going to throw my dope away and I couldn't bring it to my family's house.

I just wanted one last blast. Just one night to smoke without any of the drama. Being careful not to burn the blanket that was in the car, I pulled it over my head. I thought that I was fooling everyone. I was just fooling myself like so many times before. I told myself that no one could see me smoking in the car. After that hit I knew that I wasn't going anywhere. I think I knew that even before I took the hit. The cycle of addiction repeated itself for a total of 7 years.

Since Moosie didn't come looking for me, I got out of the car and started walking towards the house. On my way I could see someone dressed in dark clothing standing in the front yard behind a tree. I needed to get a closer look, so I slowly walked towards the house. What I saw was very disturbing. This man standing in the yard said to me in this authoritative voice, "Go back down the street." I looked around and I noticed that the entire house was surrounded. Men in full body armor and weapons drawn, was standing at every window and door. They were by the front door, the back door, in the ally, on the side of the house. There was no way out. My suspicion about Mark was right; Sharon's house was getting ready to get raided. It was going down and I couldn't get a word to anyone.

My heart began to race. I knew I had to alert someone in the house. I couldn't let this situation go down without attempting to do something. I had to try. Somehow, some way I had to find a way to call Sharon. I didn't have a cell phone back then, so I walked around in circles looking for a payphone. I found a payphone on 5th Street. My hands were trembling as I dropped the coins into the slot. When I called the house no one answered. I hung up and I called again. It felt like an eternity before the coins would land into the return slot. I called again; I still couldn't get an answer, so I called Sharon's brother.

Sharon's brother told me to go to his mother's house. I had been there once before to cut the grass with Moosie, I thought that I could find her house again. On my way, I noticed that there were a lot of yellow taxi cabs on the street that night. Way more than usual. Every five or ten minutes a taxi cab would drive slowly pass me and the driver would look slightly towards me and then look away. It looked like they were following me. Time was running out and I needed to get to Sharon's mother's house quickly without being followed. I had to do something.

So I walked up the street and down the street and up again. I was trying to make sure that I wasn't being followed; before I knew it I had walked all the way downtown to the bus station and back. I sat on someone porch trying to think about my next move. I got up and started walking to Sharon's mother house. Finally I made it. I knocked on the door. When I got inside, I told them what I saw at Sharon's house. When I walked into the next room, everyone including Sharon and her brother was listening to the police scanners, so they knew exactly what was going down. Somehow they made it out of there. It was unreal.

I told them that I think I had been followed, but I think I shook them. On my way out, someone gave me a hat and a sweater as a disguise just in case. The next day Sharon's mother's house had been raided almost immediately after I left. I found out that I had been followed. Everyone in the house said that I led the police straight there. I thought I had been real careful; that's why I walked up and down the street before I went there. That's what took me so long. This was Sharon's mother's house; I wouldn't want something terrible to happen; but they must have followed me. They must have known where I was trying to go.

The morning after the raid I went back to Sharon's house. I wanted to see if Moosie was still there. I was worried because the last time I had saw him he was in the house. I didn't know if he went to jail or what happened to him. When I got there the front door was opened and the wind was causing it to swing back and forth. I walked up to the door and peeked inside to see if anyone was there. My heart was pulsating. I was afraid to walk in. I didn't want to cross the police line. Most of all I was afraid to find evidence of a dead body. I don't know why because this wasn't that kind of bust. So I yelled "Hello." My voice echoed. I yelled again; hello, there was no answer. There were no signs of any shootings. In fact the house was completely empty. It looked as though no one had ever lived there before. It was hollow inside. Just then the task force pulled into the driveway and asked me for my identification. They told me that the house was off limits. They questioned me about the night before, but I couldn't really tell them anything, even if I could I knew that I'd better not say anything. What was I going to tell them anyway; everybody was smoking crack and that white guy Mark was an undercover cop? If he was a cop, they knew that much. They told me to leave and if I ever came back, I was going to jail. I never went back.

I called Moosie's sister C. If anyone knew where he was, she did. I was just hoping and praying that he wasn't in jail. Growing up, C and Moosie were very close. Moosie took her everywhere with him, he even took her fishing. She picked me up in her car and we went looking for him. We found him washing windshield at the 7-11. I was glad to see that he was alright. He said that he wasn't even in the house; he had left before everything went down.

We couldn't go back to the house, so we slept in the car. As I said the car wasn't running, so every night we had to push it down the block or around the corner, hoping that the rollers wouldn't tow our car or have us arrested for vagrancy.

The word on the street was that one of the alleged house guests played a major part in the Vallejo Court

House Bombing of the Records Room. People said "Big Kinney" was trying to destroy his paper trail on some case that he was facing. So he bombed the records room. Anyway I suppose they thought that he was hiding out in Sharon's house; it was bad news for us because we just happen to be renting a room at that time. I never saw him there. It was only a rumor. But that's why the house got raided.

Sharon and her sister wanted to make an example out of me. In their minds they still thought that I snitched. They found me pan handling at the Denny's Restaurant on Magazine Street and came up with the plan to say that they wanted rent money from me. Are you kidding me? It was a crack house. They said that Moosie had to pay; they couldn't find him and since I was his girl, Sharon tried to hold me responsible.

I didn't know that she felt that way about me; I thought that we were cool; in spite of everything I did try to inform her about Mark. As far as I was concerned everyone that stayed there had been evicted. I told her that I wasn't paying anything. She started yelling and getting in my face. She said she wasn't leaving until she got some money from me. She wanted me to empty my pockets. Not a fat chance. I had a little money in my pocket but I wasn't giving that up, not without a fight.

The next thing that I knew, Sharon and her sister jumped me. I couldn't fight both of them at the same time, I did my best. I grabbed Sharon by her hair and I pulled down until her head was by her knees. I wrapped my hand around her hair and somehow hooked my arm onto a pole. I grabbed onto the railing so that her sister couldn't pull me away. I had a free hand so that I could fight off her sister. I got in a couple of licks but it wasn't much I could do with one hand. Her sister took one of her high heel shoes off and started hitting me on the head. Over and over again I could feel the heel of her shoe as it tore into the flesh of my head. Blood started pouring down my face. It felt as though someone had taken a bucket of warm water and poured it over my head.

From out of nowhere Moosie came. He grabbed them away from me. Someone said that the police had been called. So we got out of there. Moosie took me to another friend's house. We called her "Mom." We went to her house a lot of times to get something to eat. She didn't have much but she always came through with something to eat. That night she gave me an ice pack for the swelling and a bandaged for my head to stop the bleeding. I couldn't go to the hospital because they would call the police and I couldn't snitch on Sharon. I wasn't afraid of her, but I was afraid of Sharon's brother.

A couple of weeks later, Sharon's brother stopped by the Arco and took me and Moosie on one of his famous rides across the Carquinez Bridge. He pulled up and said "Get in." We looked at each other and got in. we tried to explain to him what really happened.

As we crossed the bridge, on our way to Richmond, flashes of my family went through my mind. He said that we weren't coming back. I feared the worse. How will my family find my body way out here? I thought to myself, this can't be real. I thought what if I jump out of the car, what about Moosie? I can't leave him. Besides we were innocent. I tried to explain to him what really happened, how I walked up and down the street making sure that I wasn't being followed, that's why it took me so long to come to his mother's house. I told him that Sharon should have listened to me about Mark in the first place. When I saw the police outside of Sharon's house the only thing that entered my mind was that I had to protect my folks. They were my family on the street. I wanted to be the big hero and warn everyone that the house was being raided, that's really all that I was trying to do.

Moosie explained that he wasn't even home. I guess Sharon's brother was satisfied, because he turned the car around and took both of us back to the Arco and dropped us off. It was a scary situation because he had a bad reputation. At first I didn't believe all of those rumors about the type of person he was, not until we took that ride across the bridge with him. I was so terrified when Sharon's brother drove us across the bridge. I thought we would have to pay the price for something that we didn't do. Just like Jesus Christ paid the price for something he didn't do. He never sinned, yet he paid the price for the sins of this world.

It was then that I realized how grateful I was for all of those times that I washed windshields "on the house" when customers couldn't pay. I'd tell them whatever they were going to give me if they had money just place it in the offering plate at church and say a prayer for me. I needed to cash in on a couple of those prayers right now.

Jesus Christ paid the biggest price of all time. He gave His life for all mankind. He gave His life for you, and He gave His life for me. He endured great pain and suffering. Jesus' crucifixion was considered to be the most painful and degrading death one could ever endure. Yet He never said a mumbling word. Luke 24:46 says, "Thus it is written, and thus it was necessary for the Christ to suffer and to rise from the dead the third day." He hung on the Cross at Calvary for sinners like me; for repentance and the remission of sin, to anyone who will receive it.

Chapter 7

Choices

I heard the overwhelming sound of brakes squealing as the car turned the corner and the tires crushed the gravel on the unpaved road. The hair on the back of my neck stood straight up and the air flew from my lungs as the driver slowed down beside me and blew his horn. The first thing that entered my mind was that Sharon's brother was back. I thought to myself not another trip across the bridge. I turned completely around. To my surprise it was Big Moosie, he said, "Girl get in." That's when I found out that Moosie definitely had the "Gift for gab." I don't know how he did it, but he got us a van. The van needed a paint job but we didn't care about any of that as long as the roof didn't leak and the engine worked. It was great, we had shelter again.

Moosie could work wonders with that velvet tongue of his. He could talk the skin off of fried chicken. Moosie was also a people person and he loved to entertain. It didn't matter if he was getting high or not, he just loved to be around people. So he invited his friends over to celebrate our new van. With so much activity from different people coming in and out of the van, and partying all night, it became an eye sore in the neighborhood. When you're doing drugs in secret, you don't want the neighbors in your business like that.

Even though the van ran pretty good, it still had a few problems. It couldn't pass the smog inspection, so we couldn't get it registered. If we could park the van on the street legally then maybe the police wouldn't harass us as much and we'd stand a better chance of not having it towed.

We got Joe; one of those street mechanics, to work on the van. The problem with that was; he was a "crankster gangster." He smoked crank. He would be up all day, not working on the van. But because he had the tools, Moosie was willing to let him try to fix it anyway. He replaced the spark plugs, but he couldn't remember where the plug wires went, so he couldn't get the van running again; at least that's the story he told. In the morning he and Moosie planned on going to Grand Auto's to buy the parts, but Moosie had to wait for the mailman to run so he could get his S.S.I. and S.S.A. check from his step-dad's house.

There wasn't anything that Joe could do until we got the parts so he went home. We parked the van around the corner. If you think pushing a car is tough, try pushing a van. While we were waiting for Joe to show up the next day to give Moosie a ride; there was a knock on the van window. It was the police. They told us that the neighbors were complaining about the noise. In actuality the neighbors just didn't want a bunch of homeless people living on their block.

The officer gave us a break. He told us to move the van around the corner and park it at the end of Lemon Street until morning. Moosie was sure that we would be okay particularly since the officer said we could stay until morning. For a brief moment the fears of darkness and the uncertainties of not having shelter vanished as the warmth and cozy comfort from the cotton and polyester blanket shielded us from the night, but I kept thinking that something bad was going to happen. That was just me. That's how I thought. Life on the street taught me that lesson. Being able to stay without any static from the police didn't seem genuine. If it had been Officer Fernando who said we could stay then I would have believed it. But I had this feeling in the pit of my stomach. Just as I thought, when morning came, there was another knock on the window; it was the police and their barking dogs. Stone cold hearted without any sign of compassion or emotion stood the same officer who said that we could stay; now he was telling us to vacate the van immediately. And he meant immediately too. We were only allowed to take what we could carry in our arms. I was only able to grab a few items; the rest was too heavy to carry. So we had to leave the majority of our food in the van. He didn't give us any time to pack up or to grab things we needed to survive, like food, blankets, clothes. He just said that if we didn't hurry up, then we couldn't take anything. He gave us five minutes to get dressed and grab our belongings. Can you believe that? Five minutes to pack up your life. It was a cold blooded situation. We were only waiting for payday and everything was going to be fine, then most of our troubles would be over.

Nothing for us seemed to work out. Our spirits were broken. We'd tried so hard to do the right thing with the van. We were going to have it registered and everything. The lump in my throat was so large; I could hardly swallow. We just couldn't catch a break.

As we walked away from the van, I could hear the dogs barking as the sound echoed through the crisp morning air, and the chill from the cold and icy wind swept across my body. I began to shiver from the drops of rain that fell on my head, down my face, to my shoulders and along my arms as my clothes became drenched from the wet morning rain. The realization of our situation rang loud in my head; outlining a painted picture of our existence.

Once again trials and tribulations came our way. In the Psalms it talks about, there being an expectation that the answer from God will come in the morning. Often we find ourselves hindered and stagnated in having the ability to find the answers to our problems that we so desperately need. We can't wait until morning. We fell to our knees in prayer. We asked the Lord for an answer or guidance. We prayed the prayer of deliverance. We long for those sweet days of delight. We asked the Lord for His Lovingkindness. We acknowledged that in Him we trust. We ask the Lord for direction that He should guide our very steps. We cried out to him and we lifted our souls unto Him. We took shelter in the arms of God. We asked, hear our prayer O Lord. Give ear to our supplications. His Word endures forever. His Word will go forth and will not come back void. We can call upon the Name of the Lord in our times of trouble, in our times of distress. But in good times, we must prepare ourselves for the bad times. We must study and meditate on His Word day and night, that we may hide His Word within our heart so that we do not sin against Him.

That early morning we walked for blocks, wandering the street for hours, trying to figure out what our next move was going to be. Without a van I wondered where we were going to stay. It was getting colder and I was tired of walking. Moosie tried to make me feel better, he told me not to worry about it, because he was going to work something out. In the back of my mind I knew that he would. He always got us out of jams.

We decided to go to the 7-11 in Beverly Hills on Magazine Street. When we got there, we put what few things we had and placed them underneath the underpass near the 7-11. It was noisy from the cars passing by and the horns from the Big Rigs vibrated the foundation as they plowed down the road. Then we walked up the hill to the store to hustle for money. We had to hit it and quit it at the 7-11 or take the chance of going to jail. The cashier always called the police on us. At the Arco at least we washed windshields, but at the 7-11 we just asked for money. 2 Thessalonians 3:10 says, "If anyone will not work, neither shall he eat." In our own confused and distorted minds, we understood the basic principle of that scripture. That's why we earned money by washing windshield.

Even though we had permission from the owner of the Arco to wash windshields; there was a certain cashier, who we called "Bald-a-Locks." He worked the night shift. While he was on duty he wouldn't let us earn any money there. That's why we had to go to the 7-11 and take the risk and beg for money there; even if it meant that we might end up going to jail.

Later in life I realized that "Bald-a-Locks" was really trying to help us. He worked hard every day earning money, paying taxes and being a functional part of society. It seems right that he wanted us to do the same thing.

Jesus said in John 6:26-27: "Most assuredly, I say to you, you seek Me, not because you saw the sign, but because you ate of the loaves and were filled. Do not labor for the food which perishes, but for the food which endures to everlasting life, which the Son of Man will give you, because God the Father set His seal on Him."

Food that is used for human consumption satisfies the physical needs for a while, but Christ satisfies the spiritual needs forever. Amen.

The reason why the cashier at the 7-11 hated us was because our approach to making money was so aggressive, especially at night. We worked long hours in the day. We'd spend most of that money and when night came we had to make sure that we had enough money to make it through the rest of the night. I had a warrant for failure to appear, so I couldn't take the chance that the police would be called; so we had to make money quick and leave before the police came.

My warrant was because of an old situation at the convenience store on the corner of Broadway and Highway 37. I went in to buy an ice cream cone for my son and a slurpee for me, this was before I started smoking crack and abandoned my children. My son was young at the time; the ice cream cone that I was making for him spilled on the counter. It wasn't a big deal, I took the rag that was on the counter and I tried to clean it up. The cashier came over all frustrated and bothered and started arguing with me as if I spilled the ice cream on purpose. She snatched the rag out of my hand. I didn't get made right then, I just tried to explain to her that it was just a simple accident. So I gently took the rag back from her and I told her in a calm un-threatening voice that I was going to clean it up.

She got mad and picked up the "Slurpee" that I had placed on the counter and threw it on my shirt; now I was mad. I looked at her like she was crazy; before I knew it, I slapped her. Then I left the store. On my way out I picked up a soda can that was in a barrel near the front door and tossed it towards her; I missed her by a long shot. I wasn't really trying to hit her, I just wanted her to know that she had been wrong for the way she had treated me.

Before I knew it she grabbed a baseball bat from behind the counter. I rushed to my car. I tried to get in so that I could leave. I was going to go to the police station and report her for assaulting me. She and another cashier came over to where I was standing and started hitting me on my back with the baseball bat. They kept hitting me and blocking me from getting into my car.

Some guy from out of nowhere came over to help. He took the bat from the cashier's hands and stood between us to keep them from hitting me. Then he put the bat on the ground. When he did that, I swiftly picked it up. I hadn't even thought about retaliating until I saw the bat on the ground. Once I picked up the bat, both of the cashiers' started running back towards the store; just as the door was closing I hit one of them one time on the arm. Then I took the bat to the police station to report that I had been assaulted. After all, they began the actual hitting when they had beaten me with the bat several times while I was at my car.

There were no cameras outside of the store, at least not where my assault took place. The only camera was the one by the front door; the one that caught me hitting her on the arm. When I got to the police station, they brought me into the back, I made a statement. The officers left for a minute. As it turned out, while I was on my way to the police station, another officer had responded to a complaint from the cashier at the store about me. She said that I assaulted her. When the officers came back, they viewed the video tape, and then they told me that I was the one that was going to jail. "Ain't" that a trip? There weren't any cameras videotaping my assault. But there was a video tape of my hitting her on the arm. My lawyer advised me to plead no contest. This was the first time that I had been in a situation like this. I wasn't familiar with the legal process. I wasn't guilty, but by pleading no contest I was actually saying that I was. I didn't know that. I was only doing what the court appointed lawyer advised me to do. (Years later when I finally got my life together and I was trying to get a job, I went back to court to have the plea reversed so that my record could be expunged.)

Before I went to jail, I called my friend Larry to come and take my son to my parent's house. All of this over an ice cream cone. The article in the newspaper said, girl arrested over ice-cream. I guess I'll have to live with that one for the rest of my life.

After about three days in jail, I was arraigned. The judge gave me a court date. But by the time I was supposed to go back to court I had my first hit of crack cocaine at Larry's house. And I missed my court date, and a warrant was issued for my arrest.

When we would wash windshields at the 7-11, usually we could see the rollers coming up the hill, but this particular night they caught us by surprise. At first everything seemed okay; Moosie tried to use his velvet tongue when he talked to the police and it seemed as though they were going to let us go. We tried to walk away real quick, at the same time acting as if we had nothing to worry about, trying to act real casual and cool. We got about half way down the block when my warrant came over the radio. I started to run, but I changed my mind. Where was I going to run? When they put me in handcuffs, Moosie had tears in his eyes. He tried to tell me that everything was going to be alright. I wanted so desperately to believe him. I stayed in jail about ten days.

The holding officer remembered me from the first time that I went to jail. She said something that for years I hadn't realized on my own, something that I should have known and I should have seen, but I didn't. She told me that I was wasting away. By then I only weighed about 98 pounds. I was skin and bones. The physical effect that crack cocaine was having on me was shocking. My body was eating itself. I was dying from the inside out.

I hadn't realized that I was looking that bad. I had been in the game a long time and I was smoking crack cocaine every day. I had lost about 40 pounds all together. My breast had faded away. I went from about a size 36C to a training bra. I was a flat-chested, blow-pop head having, tooth pick.

When I got out of jail I called my dad to come and get me. He took me back to South Vallejo. I don't know why I didn't go home with my dad. If I had, all of my problems would have been over, because I would have been out of the game. I had many opportunities to get out of the game.

For example Pastor Richards from "Highway Church of God in Christ," who was friends with Moosie from the neighborhood Floyd Terrace, invited us to church. He never gave us money. But sometimes he would give us ink pens or tee-shirts. Anyway he would always pray for us. When he would invite us to come to church; we'd say yes with the intentions of never going. Deep down inside we wanted to go but we were too ashamed. Our clothes were torn and dirty. And we knew that everyone could tell that we were crack heads. I just couldn't face that about myself at the time. It's one thing knowing horrible things about yourself; but it's another admitting them to others. Even so this one particular time we told Pastor Richard's that we would visit his church. He made arrangements for the church van to pick us up in the morning and give us a ride. We had to explain that we actually stayed underneath the overpass by the 7-11. He didn't seem shocked and he didn't seem surprised. He just told us to be ready.

We had been up talking, strategizing, hoping and dreaming about going to church all night. We were excited; we told ourselves that tomorrow is going to be the start of something new. We were going to church and come home changed. After all that's what happens in church isn't it? Change occurs in a person's life.

I just wanted mine and Moosie's future together to be like when we first met. Back then I felt so comfortable around Moosie. I could see beyond the smoke to find comfort from a man that demonstrated compassion and heartfelt concern towards me.

When the dawn of a new day arrived and the freshness of the morning dew appeared through the dark fog, we had each other. We talked and enjoyed each other's company; dreaming and making plans for the future. Just two people, who found within themselves the ability to share a single emotion, love.

That night, the devil was busy; satan put doubts in our minds, even though we wanted to go, we found excuses not to, when God is getting ready to bless the devil really starts his mess.

When the church van pulled up to our spot we said that we weren't going, but the van driver said that he was instructed not to leave without us; after a while, we both got in the van and we went to church.

We joined the church that day. The members treated us real nice. They accepted us how we were. Isn't that what Jesus does? He accepts us as we are. Our dirty clothes didn't matter. But we allowed our own selfish pride and embarrassment stop us from going back there. For me, I don't know why but I was afraid to make the change.

Highway Church of God in Christ planted the seed, but an addict will come up with all kinds of excuses not to do the right thing. Saying that I wasn't ready to be healed was just another one of those excuses to keep doing wrong. Who doesn't want to be made whole again? If I had gone to the doctor and the doctor told me that I was going to die unless I took the medicine that he was going to prescribe, I bet you that I would take it. God was calling my name. He was saying that He wanted to heal me, take my broken spirit and make me whole again. At first I said yes. But I took one dose of the prescription and put the rest away. In reality I told God, not today.

I want to thank Pastor Richards from "Highway Church of God in Christ," for gardening, for tilling the ground and planting the seed.

Chapter 8

The Fig Tree

As we slept snuggled warmly beneath the covers, underneath the underpass, a place that we now called home, suddenly at about 3 o'clock in the morning, water from the night's rain began coming down like a flood. Our blankets, the clothes on our back, our shoes, everything was soaked through and through.

Hungry, cold, wet, and too exhausted to do anything about the water, we gathered all of our belongings and went back to the Arco Gas Station. From inside of the dumpster we grabbed some cardboard boxes and went to the porch of an old abandoned house around the corner on Fifth Street. We made ourselves a cardboard shelter and waited until morning.

My mother always said that she remembers when I was staying in a cardboard box. I've stayed in many boxed shelters while living on the street, but I've always wonder if she saw me sleeping on that porch.

When morning came the sweet sound of birds chirping on the rooftop and the warm sun shining on my face woke me up. As quickly as the rain came, the sun shone bright in the sky setting the stage for a new and exciting day.

Because Moosie needed to get the "Twisties off," he had already gone to work at the Arco. When Moosie had the "Twisties" his mouth would twist to one side. It looked as though he was going to have a stroke. He could hardly talk. Years of smoking crack cocaine affected him physically in that way.

Crack affected me physically also. I would be so tired and weak, I could hardly walk. I didn't even have the energy to wake up. Without crack, neither one of us could function very well. The devil had us stuck between a "rock" and a hard place. Rock cocaine is a hard place to be.

Every time things seemed to be at their worst, Moosie would find a way to make the situation a little easier. As I stayed asleep on the porch, Moosie hustled us a tent to stay in. As usual Moosie came to the rescue. No matter how bad things seemed to be for us, we were determined to make our situation work.

We cleared some weeds in the middle of the field under a big fig tree near the porch and pitched the tent there. Everyone could see the tent from the road. We didn't care. We had shelter and that's all that mattered. We were thankful to the Lord for His provision.

Of all the trees that could have been in that field, there was a fig tree, I thought because we were pitching our tent underneath that fig tree, it was a sign that we would have renewed prosperity by way of spiritual possessions. But we had inner turmoil within our lives and we were in the midst of a storm. The storm that we were in was a storm of the soul. Even though dark clouds hung over our face for so long, I couldn't help but to hope that our storm would soon be over. I always thought that because of the fig tree we would somehow find determination within ourselves to fight our way through and out of this devastating and troubled state of affairs.

The fig tree is different from most other fruit trees in that its fruit is green and is hidden or concealed among the leaves until it's almost time to pick.

When a fig tree is in bloom yielding its strength, in agriculture it is considered to be a sign that God has brought renewed prosperity and peace to the land. If a fig tree does not produce fruit; then it is considered to be a hypocrite.

Much like the fig tree; the good in us was hidden in our circumstances. By our own devises we were cut off from the fold, but the time would come when we would have to someday give an account and choose to produce good fruit or continue to remain cut off from the fold and be classified as a hypocrite.

We always said that we loved the Lord and maybe someday we'd stop doing what we were doing and show our love for God and live for Him, but we always convinced ourselves that because we were drug addicts that we were somehow off the hook for the moment; that we'd always have tomorrow to do the right thing.

Habakkuk 3:17-18 say, "Though the fig tree may not blossom, Nor the fruit be on the vines; Though the labor of the olive may fail, And the fields yield no food; Though the flocks may be cut off from the fold, And there be no herd in the stall-Yet I will rejoice in the Lord, I will joy in the God of my salvation."

Though our possessions were few, the spirit within us was rising to the top. In the middle of our circumstances we were experiencing the joy of the Lord. We were able to laugh and be happy because we knew that though we had little we were loved by God. And in everything and through everything, He provided for us.

Everything good or bad that happened to us we realized that the Lord was always there in the midst looking out for us. Whatever the devil meant for evil, God would always turn it into good. I know that God had a particular road for me to travel, but I was hard headed and I went my own way, but God is merciful and patient. He was leading me where He wanted me to go. All I had to do was surrender and follow.

Christmas was coming; my sister came by our spot to invite us home for our family's Traditional Christmas Breakfast. That's when I found out that my family knew that I was living in a tent in the field behind the Arco on Fifth Street; I was a little embarrassed knowing that my family could see our spot. But that didn't stop me from going home that year for Christmas.

Christmas breakfast is our family tradition. Most people have Christmas dinner, we have Christmas breakfast. Moosie declined the invitation. He said that he wanted to wait until he was more presentable. By that he meant that he wanted to wait until he had nice clothes to wear. Moosie always loved to wear nice things. But all of our clothes had been ruined from the rain.

To my family it didn't matter that our clothes were torn and dirty, or that we hadn't had a decent bath in quite a while. All that mattered was that we weren't dead, and that my family wanted me home for Christmas. But I understood why Moosie felt the way that he did. After all he really didn't know my family that well and he wanted to make a good first impression.

Christmas that year was great. It felt a little strange being with my family at first, it felt like old times but different. I was different. At this point I had experienced so many things, most of which my family could never imagine. This was my family but they had become like strangers to me and it was all my fault. We did our best to focus on the day at hand. We laughed at old times and for a moment I had forgotten all about my circumstances. They asked me to stay but I wanted to get back to Moosie. After breakfast my family drove me back to the tent at my request.

I took the gifts that my family had given to me and placed them inside of the tent. I thought my things would be safe there because all of our other things were safe. Then I went to the Arco to find Moosie.

I couldn't find him anywhere. After about an hour, I went home, when I got back to the tent, Moosie, and Brian from the Maritime Academy was sitting inside of the tent. Brian must have rolled through the Arco on Christmas Day looking to buy dope and found Moosie.

When all the dope was gone, after Moosie and Brian had smoked everything, we decided to get to work and get one last issue before settling in for the rest of the night. Since I had spent Christmas day with my family I hadn't had anything to smoke all day and I needed something to settle this nervous addiction that I was experiencing.

Brian didn't know anything about hustling, not the type of hustling that we did. He may have sold things to his friends and things like that, but not everyone can handle asking complete strangers for money, so he stayed behind in the tent. We told him to blow out the candles if he went anywhere; otherwise we would see him when we got back. We used candles to stay warm. The light from the candles also helped to keep the vermin out; we went through a box of candles a night.

Since Ball-D-Locks was working at the Arco that night, we went to the 7-11. We stayed quite a while because it was hard to make money that night. Soon we called it quits. We went down the street and bought our issue of dope. When we returned, our tent was engulfed in flames. It looked like a bon fire. We ran as close to the tent as we could without getting burned. Hysteria came upon us as we realized that Brian may still be inside, so we called out his name, but no one answered. All I could hear was the crackling sound from our things burning and the tent crumbling down. The smell was horrible. It smelled like death.

The Fire Department came and put out the fire. Fortunately, no one was inside of the tent. All we could do was to watch our tent burn to the ground along with everything that we owned including all of my Christmas gifts. All we had were the clothes on our back, once again. We couldn't do anything about it but try to carry on with our lives. At least we were still alive. The next day we tried sifting through the debris, but there was nothing left but remnants of our past.

    I expected to see Brian the next day, after all he was there when we left and the fire was no secret. The flames could be seen all over Fifth Street. But he was nowhere to be found. I believe in my heart that he started the fire to cover up the fact that he stole my Christmas gifts. After that night we never saw him again. He played us for a Sucker. I used to think about him and if he was able to live with himself. You can't get any lower than stealing from a homeless person. All that was left was the story of our misfortune; everything else had been destroyed. True tragedy makes for a good hustle. So we made the most out of our tragedy. Most people will help if they believe that the situation is real and ours was real. Our customers really came through for us.

Chapter 9

Blowing Smoke

After our tent had burned down, we did what we had to do; we broke into the garage of the house next to the field where our tent was and moved in. At night it was really cold inside. The area was very spacious, approximately 40 by 50 feet. There was no electricity so we didn't have any heat. In order to stay warm we took unused portions of motor oil from containers that people threw away, then we saturated old newspapers with the oil, and then we placed the paper on a tree stump that we found in the field and lit the paper on fire.

Smoke filled the room; we could hardly breathe, so we kept the garage doors partially open. I can only imagine the toxic fumes that came from burning oil and newspaper. The things we did in order to stay warm. From the outside you could see trails of smoke roll onto the garage door and upwards towards the roof. It looked as though the garage was blowing smoke. It's amazing that no one called the fire department.

Our life in the garage was dangerous. I'm surprised that we didn't burn ourselves up or die from smoke inhalation. It was here I believe Moosie developed a problem with his lungs - years later he died. Between smoking crack cocaine, smoking cigarettes, and breathing in those toxic fumes it's a wonder that I don't have lung cancer or emphysema myself.

When I first met Moosie, he was always doing push-ups and back arms; he loved to exercise. Every time we'd come to the end of a block; he would knock out about 50 push-ups and 50 back arms. He covered about ten or eleven blocks every day. Just imagine how many push-ups and back arms he did during the day. Years later; he started getting winded. I could see him deteriorating. I believe his difficulty breathing had a great deal to due with the combination of the toxic smoke inside of the garage and smoking crack.

Physical effects were only one aspect of our problems. Sometimes Moosie would have a psychological reaction to the hit that he had just taken. I remember we were smoking inside of the garage when he sat down beside me. He took his hand and started moving it around the silhouette of my body; he was looking for another guy. He did this to me a lot. It drove me nuts. I could never understand how in his mind he thought he saw or heard another guy in the room with us. When he started tripping like that it was nothing that I could do. He was going to see what he wanted to see. I don't know what got into me but I decided to teach Moosie a lesson. So I got up and went to the back of the garage. I knew that he thought that there was another guy back there, so I played along with his paranoia. When I got to the back, just as I had predicted Moosie thought that another guy was there with me.

We started arguing about it, just then; Moosie picked up an empty 40 ounce bottle of beer and threw it towards me. He hit me so hard in the face with the beer bottle that I fell to my knees. I took my hand, placed it over my face. All I could feel was a pool of blood from my nose streaming down into the palm of my hand. I thought that I was going to pass out.

When Moosie saw what he had done I suppose he felt ashamed. He grabbed hold to my arms and stood me to my feet, and then he took me to the Arco. The cashier gave me some bandages and I cleaned up in the bathroom. He wasn't really trying to hurt me. I think he was trying to hit that guy that he imagined in his mind.

When we are filled with the guilt of our sin; we can get caught up in doing wrong things. We start blaming others for our misconceptions of the situation and allow them to over-shadow what is really happening in our lives. Evil ways creates its own circumstances, but we don't have to be victims because of them. Yes we were homeless and yes we were drug addicts, but that didn't mean that we had to stand still and allow satan to destroy our souls. Our hearts were filled with such destruction and we felt so guilty inside because we had rebelled against the Lord; we blamed each other, therefore we tried to destroy each other.

Later the garage became infested with smoke fumes and garbage from all of the ash and trash we left behind, forcing us to move out. We didn't have to go very far only upstairs. We broke one of the windows on the back door and forced our way in.

Everyday we brought in buckets of water from the Chevron Gas Station so that we could wash up and have water to flush the toilet. By pouring water into the toilet bowl it provided us with the capability to flush the toilet. In order to solve our other utility problem we used candles for warmth and electricity.

Outside we set up a Bar-B-Que pit so that we could cook our food. The word got out, among other homeless friends, so we had a picnic. A couple of friends stated that they needed a place to stay so we opened the house. We only used the Living Room because trying to keep all the bedrooms in the house warm by candles was a challenge. We put up patricians made of sheets to divide the space and make a room for everyone. For a time, life was pleasant.

In my mind's eye I can see her; one of Moosie's old friends from back in the day. Her name was "Gay," For lack of a better word; I'll call her the lady of seduction. She needed a place to stay; so we let her stay with us.

One afternoon, after hustling at the Arco all morning long, I went back to the house. I walked into the living room; all I could see was red. Someone had a battery operated radio and the music was playing.

Gay was dancing and trying to entice my man Moosie. The only thing missing was a stripper pole. This was the second time that I had caught her dancing like that. I had warned her before. The next thing I knew, I had grabbed her by the hair and pulled her to the ground. I put her in a "head lock." Then I asked Moosie the question as I held her to the ground, "Me or her, choose now!" I told him. "She's got to go or you'll never see me again." That was the last time that I saw Gay.

I was angry with Moosie more than I was with her, because, I asked Moosie in the beginning if they had ever been more than friends. He lied and claimed that nothing was going on between them. It sure looked like something was going on to me. All I know is that this was the second time in our relationship that I questioned Moosie's loyalty to me.

Later we found out that Eradge who owned the Arco had bought the property where we were staying. He was going to "flip" the house. He was going to gut out the entire house and rebuild. Somehow he knew that we were staying there; so he told us that we had about a month before we had to leave. Our stay there was short and sweet.

When the month was up, we moved next door into the neighbor's garage. They let us rent the garage from them for five dollars a day. We couldn't beat that price. I could make five dollars with my eyes closed. There wasn't any running water; we were use to that. But we did have electricity. We had a real bed and a television set too. I couldn't believe it. For the first time in years I could watch TV. I almost stopped hustling at the Arco, at least for a day anyway. But all good things must come to an end. I had to make that five dollars.

As time passed; we became friends with Eradge; the owner of the Arco. He told me he could see how we helped his business. You see the fact that we had regular customers played a major part in changing his opinion about us. When customers came to the gas station looking for us to wash their windshields, they would spend lots of money inside of the store as well, while we pumped their gas and washed their windshields; so it was a win, win situation. Most of our customers were Baller's (drug dealers) anyway, and that's how we conducted business. Being able to work at the Arco made it that much easier to earn money to pay for the garage we rented also.

Soon Eradge began giving me odd jobs around the Arco. Cheap labor if you will. I got five dollars for most jobs like keeping the parking lot clean, flattening empty cardboard boxes inside of the dumpsters, changing the price on the billboard sign that displayed gas prices, stocking merchandise inside of the store for five dollars. I even cleaned the restrooms and stripped and waxed the floor. He gave Moosie ten dollars to wash his Lexus. Yes he let him wash his Lexus. We were drug addicts, but basically we had an honest hustle. We worked for ours.

Washing Eradge's Lexus was the start of a new hustle for us. We began a small car washing hustle using the Arco's water. For five dollars, you could get the outside of your car washed; for ten dollars, you could get the full treatment; we'd clean the inside and wash the outside of your car and detail it like new money.

Eradge was a hustler too. He even taught me how to change the gas nozzles after customers would accidentally drive off with the nozzle still in their gas tank. Eradge kept replacement parts inside of the store. He only paid me five dollars for the work. I know that it would have cost much more if he had to call the company to do the repair. But money is money.

After I became real good at doing the repairs we incorporated that job into our hustle. Sometimes we would pre plan a "drive off," that's when customers would pretend that they forgot that they had the gas nozzle in their tank and accidentally drive off. No one could prove if it was an accident or not, that was the good thing about it. I'd replace the nozzle just so we could make five dollars. We did that when our drug connection was ready to leave and we were short of money and needed to cop right then, so we pre planned a drive off. Even still Eradge, treated us like family. One time he took us to Yard Birds to buy a "Weed Eater" and a "Leaf Blower." He hired us to clean the Arco parking lot and to manicure the shrubbery on the hill side of the Arco by Fifth Street. He paid us $50 a month to do that job. It might not sound like a lot of money but it was guaranteed money. Eradge got more bang for his buck. He made more off of the jobs we did for him than he paid us, but I have to remember, if it wasn't for him we wouldn't have been able to work at the Arco at all.

Since we worked for Eradge now; when we were there, we kept the rift raft out. We wouldn't let anyone else hustle there, that was our spot. Favor once again was playing a major role in our lives. Even though we were drug addicts we had the sense to know that God was setting the foundation in our lives. We knew that change was inevitable. God loved us so much; He never gave up on us.

Other times when we had a hard time making money, there were other hustles that got us through. Some we did by our own creative devices and others we did by opportunities that came our way. The place where we pitched our tent was also where we made money. People paid us to dump certain items like Big Rig tires, couches, refrigerators, anything that normally needed to be disposed of at the city dump we allowed them to dump in the field. Then we would turn right around and get paid by Eradge to take the items to the dump yard. We used a friend's truck. We had a nice hustle going on. The cold thing about it was that we had the owner's permission to be on his property and the police couldn't do anything about that, even though they tried.

One night the "Task Force" pulled up to the Arco and told me that I would be washing my last windshield, the officer told me that I had to leave. I was shocked. I tried to make it clear that I had the owner's permission but he didn't want to hear what I had to say.

The officer went inside of the store expecting the cashier to agree with him, instead he got the shock of his life; the cashier explained everything to him and I was able to stay. So I got kind of cocky with the officer and I told him to kick rocks. I don't know what gave me the courage to do that but before I could stop myself the words came out of my mouth. He got mad and searched all of my personal belongings looking for drugs or drug paraphernalia; but that night; lucky for me, he didn't find anything. That's really why he was there; he wanted to find a reason to arrest me, I'm sure of it. You know the police know who's doing what in their neighborhood; it's just a matter of time before they decide they want you; when they do, they'll come and get you. The "Task Force" thought that they could scare me into giving them information if they threatened me with being arrested. They couldn't arrest me that night, but I knew they would try again.

Officer Fernando wasn't like that. I respected him, because he respected us. He had a heart of gold. If he told us that it was time to go, that's what we did because he treated us like real people. In the winter, he'd bring us gloves to keep our hands warm, or food to eat. Not just any food- crab or shrimp. "The good stuff." Once he even gave me this big warm FUBU jacket in the middle of winter. Can you believe that? It was nice.

I went to the Chevron and tried it on. That's where we started washing up. Rather than toting water in a bucket from the Chevron to the house every day.

Before I tried the jacket on, I looked in the mirror; I had forgotten who I was. I no longer looked like me. But it was me in the mirror. I was someone's daughter, someone's sister, and most of all I was someone's mother. All I could see was that I had lost so much weight that the coat swallowed me up. But it kept me warm.

It hurts me knowing that I can never get those seven precious years back. My children had to deal with both the emotional pain of me not being there and the physical pain of seeing what was happening to me. I allowed satan to attack my mind. I convinced myself that I needed to get high in order to function. If only I could have found the strength to allow time to heal me. As long as I kept putting the poison into my body, I was going to have a negative physical reaction. My physical reaction was mega weight loss.

One night I was so hungry, I had been up all night getting high. I hadn't eaten at all that day. In fact I couldn't remember the last time I had eaten anything. The time was 3 o'clock in the morning; early morning; what my mother calls, morning before day. I called my Parents home, my mother answered. I told her that I was hungry. I asked her to please bring me some food. She got up out of her warm bed and brought me something to eat. I had forgotten what a home cooked meal tasted like. My belly was full for the night. I called my mother on many occasions, each time she would come. No matter what time of the night and no matter how difficult it was for my mother to see me living on the street, she came.

I'm not trying to glorify any of my drug addicted behavior. My hope is that by reading about my experiences, and the grief that I caused my family, others won't even entertain the thought of using drugs. And if they are, maybe these words will inspire them to stop.

In life, everyone has had to overcome some type of difficulty. I spent seven years on the streets of Vallejo, homeless and addicted to crack cocaine. My addiction was the beginning of pain and agony for my family.

The Bible says we shall have trials and tribulations. I must continue to say that I am an expert witness of the power that Jesus Christ has, for He delivered me from the binding effects of crack cocaine.

My loved ones are still dealing with the emotional effects that I caused from the choices that I made in my life. Look at all the time that was lost with my family because of my selfishness.

If we as so called Christians would do our part in seed sowing then the unsaved homeless person can expect to have hope for tomorrow. But we would rather pass a homeless person up because we see them with a beer in their hands and we tell ourselves that's all they're going to do with the money if we give it to them. We don't even give them the choice to choose. We assume that they already know Jesus Christ and decided to turn away. But how will they know if we don't tell them. We don't even take the time to ask them their name; let alone pray for them. We would rather act as if they didn't even exist; so that we don't have to feel guilty about what we are not doing.

Chapter 10

Three Days For The Rest Of My Life

Tears rolled down my face. My heart filled with joy, and hope abided within my soul. All of my years of hoping and praying for deliverance had finally come. And I knew that my life's circumstances were truly under God's control.

My daughter had driven all the way from Visalia, CA, to share some amazing and wonderful news with me. She told me that she was pregnant. Wow, I said to myself. I was going to be a grandmother for the first time. A feeling of triumph exploded from within me. It was at this moment in time that I had begun to experience the joy of forgiveness. For me to have this amazing gift from God meant only one thing; the pathway to redemption had begun.

I knew that I couldn't be an addict and a grandmother at the same time. It was time to admit defeat, lay down my pride and surrender my life's circumstances to the Most High God, The Alpha and The Omega, The Beginning and

The End, The God of my Refuge, The God of my Strength, The God of my Salvation. I also knew that if I were going to depend on God to help me, it was going to require complete commitment on my part. This meant that I had to totally trust in God and allow myself to give myself to the Lord for His safekeeping. It was then that God placed a sense of urgency upon my life. He enabled me while in my recovery phase to remain steady in the faith, a faith that in the past I had only hoped and dreamed of. I now understood the scripture when it says: I can do all things through Christ who strengthens me. Alone I could do nothing, but with Christ's help I knew that I could make it. I've known this during my entire addiction, but I wasn't willing or ready to surrender. I thought I was in control.

God promises that if we submit to His timing, he will honor us, and if we humble ourselves under God's mighty hand, He will lift us up in due time. I had to learn to allow God to choose the best time to change my circumstances. And the time was now. Growing up I've always heard that God is an on time God. Yes He is. I'm a witness.

1 Peter 5:6-11 says, Therefore humble yourselves under the mighty hand of God, that He may exalt you in due time, casting all your cares upon Him, for He cares for you. Be sober; be vigilant; because your adversary the devil walks about like a roaring lion, seeking whom he may devour. Resist him, steadfast in the faith, knowing that the same sufferings are experienced by your brotherhood in the world. But may the God of all grace, who called us to His eternal glory by Christ Jesus, after you have suffered a

while, perfect, establish, strengthen, and settle you. To Him be the glory and the dominion forever and ever. Amen.

For years I allowed satan to attack me with his cunning and cruel ways. He fooled me for such a long time. I gave in to his deceptions. But through Christ Jesus I am commanded not to run from satan any longer, rather to resist him, to stand and fight; never to flee from him. When we remain committed to God, victory will come to us. God is greater than our enemy satan. He will give us the ability to overcome if we would only submit to His will.

I desperately needed Him to show me the right way to go. God offers help for today and hope for tomorrow. We can trust God to give us both the peace and the strength to weather the storms of life. If I was ever going to get out of my situation, I needed help from the Lord.

Psalm 25:8-9 says, Good and upright is the Lord; therefore he instructs sinners in His ways, he guides the humble in what is right and teaches them His way. As we trust in God He grants our request; often in ways that we can't even imagine. What the devil means for evil, God will turn it into good. As such was the case in our dealings with our friend Kurt.

Kurt was a suit wearing Caucasian gentleman who came through the hood looking for "yayo" I met him at the Arco one day while I was washing windshields. I could tell that he had money to spend and I knew that he was going to have to be served "proper," So I introduced him to Big Moosie. He saw to it that Kurt got served "fat."

Kurt became one of our regular customers. At first glance you would never think that he was a smoker. They say never judge a book by its cover. When Kurt came to the Arco, the party was on. He spent hundreds of dollars at a time and we knew that the rest of the night would be easy for us. When Kurt came through, we didn't have to wash windshield the rest of the day.

By working with Kurt, I developed a system known as "The Contract." When we contacted our source on the phone, we'd just tell him how many contracts we wanted.

Let me break it down like this. Each contract was worth $50. Kurt would spend at least $200 at a time, (the price of four contracts, or four "50 pops"). We gave Kurt the two fattest 50 pops (or $100 worth) and we told him that we paid $200. We kept the other two 50 pops as payment for our services. Kurt never knew anything about the term contracts. As far as, he knew we gave him $200 worth of crack.

The contracts were our "Come Up." Kurt became our friend and foe at the same time, but in the game, that's how the hustle goes; no crack head in their right mind would ever go out on a limb and not reap some of the benefits. That would be an oxymoron to even think that a crack head can be 100% loyal. The only thing that Kurt needed to know was that he got served proper. We made sure of that. We served him the "cream," the good stuff. The devil must have felt that he had us in the ultimate trap. Here was a customer with big money to spend. The devil must have felt that he had us hemmed up for life by keeping us distracted with the contracts.

After we took a couple of hits, we'd re-bag the two "50 pops" that we held back for ourselves into dime bags and sell them back to Kurt when he came through again. We knew that after the cream that we served him, he was definitely coming back. We made money and dope without spending a dime of our own money. That's how we smoked for free. We used the money that we made from dealing with Kurt to purchase a room so we could take a decent shower. Every time Kurt came through it was like payday.

One day Kurt rolled through the Arco. Moosie having the gift for gab, made some kind of deal with him. Kurt was going to give him $300 to buy this mobile home that was parked in the Motel 6 parking lot near the Arco. The Mobile Home had been sitting in the parking lot for quite a while. Moosie wanted to buy it from the manager who wanted to sell it for $400. Moosie only had about $100 left from his SSI check. Kurt helped us with the rest. It was strictly business.

I know that Kurt had to get something out of the deal too, so we served him the dealers special. We served him how we were used to being served; and that was fat. Kurt got served the whole contract. When he saw the issue he was very happy.

Even though we did the best that we could with the tools that we had to make our fort secure; let's get real, no matter how much time and effort we put in to making the fort livable, no one wants to live like that forever. Getting the Mobile Home meant that we wouldn't have to worry about the rain getting in. It also meant that we wouldn't have to sleep in the fort anymore.

The fort was in a spot behind the Chevron Gas Station next to the bridge in South Vallejo. We built it after we left the neighbor's garage when the police forced us to leave because it became a crime scene, because the dead body of a young man was found on the street.

We used tree branches and other things from nature to build our fort so that we could have a place to stay. We had to get shelter up in a hurry because it was getting dark.

Later Moosie got a bunch of lumber; he was good at hustling things like that; we used the lumber to make our fort sturdy. It looked like a shack, but it did the job. It kept the wind and the rain away. We covered it with blankets and blue tarp then we used trees to camouflage it so that it couldn't be seen from the road.

The body lying in the street belonged to this young cat who we bought dope from time to time. In my opinion he didn't belong in the game. He was one of those young guys who I felt had great potential. He talked about going back to school so that he could help take care of his family. I can't say if he was out there selling drugs or anything on the night of his death; I only saw him selling drugs every now and then. He seemed like a very nice guy, clean cut, well mannered. He just didn't fit the profile of a drug dealer.

I tried to replay that morning in my mind a thousand times. When I left to go to the Arco, I don't remember seeing a body lying on the street. It was too dark out when I left. Maybe it was so dark because the street lights were out. I just didn't notice if he was there when I left. But in those days I never wore my glasses either; I lost them years earlier. I never even heard gun shots or anything that night.

Yet, the young man still lost his life. I suppose he did what he felt he had to do at that particular time in his life.

No one knows for sure except the killer. I'm upset at myself because I was raised in the church. I wished that I could have been less involved in my addiction and taken the time to really talk to this young man about Jesus. I only hope and pray that he knew Jesus for himself. I just know that none of us can judge who will make it into Heaven and who won't. Only God knows.

This young man lost his life. I often wonder what would have happened if he'd had just a little more time. We will never know. I only know that since I was going to become a grandmother I was faced with the need to make an immediate decision in my life. I could no longer say I'll decide tomorrow, because tomorrow was here.

God promises to forgive us and He delivers us from sin's eternal consequences, but we still must face the worlds consequences. It might not be today and it might not be tomorrow, but one day we will have to deal with the consequences of the choices that we make in life. But know that God will give us the strength to conquer.

When I took that first hit of crack cocaine, I never stopped to think about what could happen to me. And I never stopped to think about what would happen to my children. In fact I was one of those people who said that it could never happen to me; I'm different.

It's amazing the choices that we make in life. I chose homelessness. No one forced that lifestyle upon me, I chose it. I abused by body through years of drug addiction and because of it I found myself staying places that most people could only imagine. I even found myself eating food left in garbage cans. Something that I could never imagine, but I did it to survive. There is no glamour in the life of an addict.

Let me share a story that Pastor Brown of Saint Mark in Vallejo, CA told me. There was a man who had fallen into a deep hole. No matter how hard he tried; he couldn't find his way out. People passed by the man in the hole; as he yelled for help. They'd look at him and would keep on going.

One day a certain man passed by; he saw the man in the hole and asked him, "How did you get yourself in that hole. The man replied, I thought that I saw something in the hole that I wanted, so I climbed into the hole. When I got to the bottom of the hole, I discovered that what I thought I saw was not real; and I didn't need it nor could I use it. Then the man in the hole said, but this hole is too deep and I can't climb out of it. Can you help me?

So this certain man replied, yes of course I can. And he climbed down into the hole with the man.

This man who had been in the hole was furious. He said how can you help me now? We are both in the hole together.

But the certain man said you see I've been in this hole before. I can show you the way out of the hole."

When I made up my mind to surrender my addiction to the Lord; I was able to climb out of my hole. Let me help you crawl out of your hole? I never looked back with regret. When I do look back; it's with thanksgiving. I know how far I had fallen.

I sold my soul into bondage. I bound myself to the contracts of this world. There is one called Jesus, who took upon Himself my contract. He rewrote it in His precious Blood. Because of Him I was set free.

I imagined life being different having a mobile home. I dreamed of decorating it and making it really look like a home. It needed a lot of work inside and out, much like my life. I needed a lot of work inside and out. But just like we bought the mobile home anyway, Christ Jesus paid for our sins anyway.

Moosie got another one of those "street mechanics," to do the engine work, and I started gathering all kinds of wallpaper and plants, anything that I could find to make it look and feel like a home. It took a long time for the mechanic to fix everything, but he finally got it running and I was happy.

Since we weren't paying guests, the manager of the Motel wasn't going to let us camp out in his parking lot for an indefinite period of time, especially since our mobile home was an eye sore, so we had to move it quickly.

Moosie's step father was named Mr. Scott, he lived in Beverly Hills and he said that it was ok to park our mobile home in his yard as long as we paid rent. His step father worked all of his life. I think he was a pipe fitter or something like that. Even in his retirement, he would get up early in the morning and collect recyclables. He brought in about $250 a month from that. Everything that Moosie's stepfather did was huge. He was a great man with a big heart.

It was quite a sight and an adventure at the same time, driving the mobile home to Moosie's step dad's house. When we cranked it up for the first time, there was a hole in the muffler, it sounded like bats trapped in a barrel. The motor was loud, plus it didn't have any brakes. Unfortunately we found that out after we were already on the road. When Moosie pressed on the brakes, nothing happened. He shouted "hold on and watch your head." Everything inside of the mobile home began sliding back and forth. Each time we'd make a turn, I'd lose my balance and the cabinet doors would swing open and everything inside would fall out.

Finally we made it to the house without getting a ticket or getting into an accident. We parked at Moosie's stepfather's house. It was at this point in life that God used Kurt to help us purchase the mobile home. Without the mobile home I wouldn't have been in the position that I needed to be in when my daughter came by to tell me that she was pregnant. I would have been living in the fort just existing without any of the comforts of life. The mobile home gave us a little more stability. Having the mobile home allowed me to see my life differently. I began to dream again.

I knew that I had to stop using drugs. I didn't want to walk down the street holding my grandson's hand while I was still using drugs. I didn't want the dealer to approach me about buying any amount of drugs. I didn't want my grandson to see or hear anything about that lifestyle.

Life is short. We must never put off things that we can change for what we think will be better suited for another day. Sometimes we are faced with having to make the most important decisions in our lives without delay. For one more moment in time wasted on sinful selfish desires can and often leads to tragic unchangeable outcomes. That young man found dead in the street might have been faced with such a dilemma.

The joy that I felt knowing that I was going to become a grandmother could not be expressed in mere words. I was so thankful and grateful that I didn't succeed with my suicide attempts. I would have lost out on the greatest blessing of all. I never want to feel like that again ever in life. Never to have known my grandchildren Jason and Kamil would have been the biggest mistake of my life.

I told everyone in the house that I was going to quit using. They didn't really believe me; after all it wasn't the first time that I'd said I was quitting. But this time it felt different. In order to live, I needed to quit just like I needed air to breath. I needed to inhale God's Grace on my life and exhale His Plan for my life.

I didn't think that I would have a problem quitting; but it was more difficult than I thought. Anything worth having is worth fighting for. I realized that having the Lord on my side to help me win this fight, this battle, this war, is all that I needed. It made the fight to survive easy. I didn't really know how easy the fight would be with the help of the Lord.

A year prior, I made my second suicide attempt when we stayed at the Economy Lodge near the bowling alley off of Magazine Street. Shortly after Moosie's payday while his pockets were still fat. Moosie invited his "crankster" friend Mike over. He offered us some crank. Of course I said no. I was scared to smoke crank just like I was scared to smoke heroine. Mike heated up the crank with a lighter, and then he took a needle and placed it into the spoon, and extracted the liquid. Mike took a tie and put it around his arm, as his vein bulged, he injected the crank into it.

After a few minutes, Mike and Moosie left. Since I didn't smoke any crank, I was still feigning for a hit of crack, so I opened every drawer in the room looking for crack. I looked in Moosie's pants pockets. I looked under the bed. I got down on my hands and knees and combed the carpet hoping to find anything. Just a crumb, that's all I needed. I looked everywhere, but I couldn't find anything. Finally Moosie and Mike walked through the door, but the only thing that they had was some more crank.

Words can not express how angry and disappointed I felt. I told Mike to give me some of that crank anyway. I was going to show them. They weren't going to stop me from getting high. I needed a hit of crack but the crank was going to have to do. Mike got the tools together and prepared everything for me. I let him inject that poison into my arm. That was the first and last time that I ever used crank. I stood there motionless as splashes of sparkles flashed in front of my eyes.

I went over to the bed and shook Moosie on his arm. "Get up" I told him. "I gotta get this feeling off me." I felt weird. It was like a psychedelic movie. I told him that he was going to have to get me some weed or something, because whatever was happening to me, I didn't like it. Plus, the way that I was feeling, I couldn't allow myself to be hooked on crank too. I didn't like being a crack head and I surely didn't want to be a crankster. All of the cranksters that I knew had sores on their face from smoking that stuff. Anyway the high was wack.

Hours had passed and Moosie and Mike weren't back yet. I looked on the table and I saw Moosie's 40 ounce bottle of "2-11," so I turned it up and took a big swig. I took a Gerber jar that was used as a pipe and scrapped the residue of crack cocaine out of it and made myself a hit. Normally that would be a nice hit if I had some more dope to go with it. But I didn't. That didn't stop me from trying. That crack residue didn't counter act my crank high.

The next thing that I remember, I was sitting inside of the closet of the Motel room facing the front door. I was still "tripping" off the crank high. I was having a bad "trip." I did not like that high. It made me extremely distraught. I paced the room for hours in a state of hysterical depression before I got into the closet. My life flashed in front of me and I imagined my family seeing me not only hooked on crack cocaine but now I was going to be hooked on crank. I wasn't going to let that happen. Not that! Anything but that! I took the belt from Moosie's robe and I tied it on the back bar inside of the closet. Then I took a chair and placed it inside of the closet so that I could sit down. I put the belt around my neck then I sat down and leaned back in the chair making the rope tight around my neck. I had positioned myself in such a way that if I passed out after drinking the rest of that "40" then the chair would fall from under me and I would hang, killing myself. I was determined to do precisely that. I had a razor blade in my hand and I made a couple of superficial cuts on my arm. I was trying to get the nerve to make a real deep cut, one that would matter.

I know that I wanted to die. I couldn't become a crankster. I thought about the time before, when I attempted suicide and how my attempt didn't work. This time I was by myself. There were no neighbors to call the police.

I felt defeated after I took that hit of crank. I tried to reverse my high by drinking that beer and taking that little hit of residue. When that didn't work, I felt ashamed. I didn't want anyone to see me like that. I didn't know what to do. I felt as though I didn't have any way out. I was literally at the end of my rope.

I sat in the chair with the belt around my neck and a razor blade in my hand, waiting for anything to happen. Tears were rolling down my face. I was crying and "blubbering" about how bad things in my life had gotten. In the back of my mind I wanted Moosie to walk in and stop me or something. Maybe I just wanted him to find me dead, only God knows.

When I woke up the next morning, I was lying in bed, I had bruises all over my chest and I had a cut on my left arm. Moosie said that he and Mike had to throw water on me to try to wake me up. When that didn't work they had to pound my chest. He said that they had to do CPR on me. I was listening to the words that Moosie was saying but, it all felt so unreal.

I couldn't remember any of that, but I do remember taking a razor blade and making shallow marks across my arm trying to get the courage to cut deep. I must have passed out, because I don't remember making that final cut on my arm. Fortunately, I didn't hit a major vein or anything but I did cut deep enough to leave a 2 ½ inch scare that I still have today. I never tried crank again. I'd rather be dead.

Sometimes that night seems unreal, as though it never happened, but I have the scar to prove it. That's how I know that it wasn't a dream. Crack made me feel bad about myself and the choices that I had made in life, but crank made me want to end my life for real. It brought to surface the devastating reality of my condition. I can only say that I thank God for my life.

Remembering the way that I lived back then is the motivating factor that encourages me to share my life with you today; God saw something in me that's worth saving and sharing. It's the same thing that He sees in you. Know that there is hope in the Everlasting God. That hope is available to all who believe.

My life was spinning out of control. And I was feeling mental pressures. It was time to make a change. I couldn't go on living like this. I had spent too many years ripping and running from the Lord, it was time to let go and let God. I needed Him to move into my life and take complete control. I needed Him to guide me in the right direction.

Proverb 3:5-6: Trust in the Lord with all your heart, and lean not to your own understanding, in all your ways acknowledge Him, and He shall direct your path. I definitely needed the Lord's guidance. Not now but right now. I couldn't get out of my situation alone. I knew that I needed to totally surrender my life into the Lord's hands. It took a long time to come to this conclusion. But I was willing to finally try. For real this time I was going to quit smoking.

Everyone in the house was smokers including me. But now I was trying to become an ex-smoker. When the reality about me really trying to quit set in and that I was serious this time; the problems in the household began. The next day I was washing windshield at the Arco; but I wasn't buying dope.

I had a few dollars in my pocket. I knew that if I didn't buy any dope then I would have to buy something to eat. If I didn't have something to eat; I knew that I would buy dope. I wanted to hang onto my money just in case I got the strength to go to the store to buy something to eat later that night; after all the 7-11 was open all night and we only lived about 3 miles away.

I was winning; I hadn't bought any dope all day. For someone who used to smoke all day every day; even one day not smoking took a lot of strength and determination on my part. In order to stop smoking just for one day would require every ounce of concentration and every bit of strength that I had. The urge to smoke was great. The struggle inside of me was strong.

You can't stay in a dope house with money in your pocket and not buy dope. Not if other people know that you have money. People started getting mad at me; they wanted dope; but didn't have any money. I had money but didn't want any dope. This was a new experience for me. I knew in order not to feel so tired and exhausted all I needed to do was to smoke some dope. But I knew that I couldn't do that. What would my daughter say when she saw me again. I was afraid that she would never let me see my grandson when he was born.

I was so tired and weak from not smoking. All I wanted to do was to eat and sleep. All those years of smoking had taken a toll on my body; one day clean seemed like a lifetime. I was so exhausted from not smoking. Staying clean took all of the energy and will power that I had.

I sat down next to Moosie and I explained to him why I wanted to quit smoking and what it was going to take in order for me to be successful. I told Moosie that the only thing I needed was three days of sleep. Three days for the rest of my life I told him.

I wanted to get clean really bad. I was going to be a grandmother. This was going to be my chance to make a change in my life. It was something about the way that I was looking at him and he was looking at me that he realized how important this was to me. For the first time all day I felt as though he really understood my dilemma.

I think it was Wednesday or Thursday and I was on my second day clean when my daughter came by again to invite me to Visalia, CA. for the weekend. Now I really had to stay clean for my daughter and my unborn grandson, but Moosie kept bothering me, especially since he had the "Twisties."

He tried to leave me alone but his "Twisties" were really bad that day, they were getting so bad that he wanted to fight me for my money. I only had about ten dollars. I don't think either one of us really understood the impact of quitting smoking would have on the way we conducted business. That is the business of windshield washing. I imagine that he understood that I would be quitting, but he might have thought that I would still help him wash windshield to make money to get rid of his "Twisties." But once I realized how tired I was, all I wanted to do was sleep it off. We had worked together for so long, we depended on each other to come through during the others weak point of the day; my being tired and Moosie's "Twisties."

When an addict has come to the point in life when they have decided it is time to quit using drugs, anything could cause a relapse. Their will power is vulnerable. It's a difficult time. That's why most addicts try to sleep it off. The less interaction we have with people the better. The less conflicts during this time, the easier it is to make it to the next day clean. When people say one day at a time, it really takes that.

Because of all the arguing with Moosie that day I finally gave in and used my money so Moosie could get rid of his "Twisties." I couldn't just buy drugs with my money and not get part of the "Issue." If I was going to use my money to buy dope; I was going to smoke too. That's the way it was.

I don't blame Moosie; there have been a lot of times when he tried to sleep his "Twisties" off and I wouldn't leave him alone because I needed to get my "tired off."

I was really disappointed in myself because I didn't make it passed my second day of being clean. What was I going to do now? I asked myself. My big weekend with my daughter was coming up and all I could think about was how I failed to stay clean.

I felt ashamed and I started to cry. I told C that I wasn't going to Visalia. I told her that I couldn't go there in the condition that I was in. She reminded me how much I really wanted to spend time with my daughter and she made me realize that I needed to go. It didn't matter that I smoked the night before. She told me that it was o.k. She said that it wasn't the end of the world and that I could try again. Then she helped me pack a few clothes.

The devil wanted me to fail. If it had not been for C I might not have gone to Visalia when I did. And I would probably be still using drugs or dead; thank you C and thank you Lord.

When Friday, May 4, 2001 came, I went with my daughter for the weekend to Visalia, CA. I didn't realize it then but I was finally going to get what I had been asking for. Three days for the rest of my life.

Psalms 31:1-5 says, In You, O Lord, I have taken refuge; let me never be put to shame, deliver me in your righteousness. Turn your ear to me, come quickly to my rescue; be my rock of refuge' a strong fortress to save me. Since you are my rock and my fortress, for the sake of your name, lead and guide me. Free me from the trap that is set for me, for You are my refuge. Into Your hands I commit my spirit; redeem me, O Lord, the God of truth.

When we got to Visalia, my daughter grabbed a CD from the glove compartment of her car. She said, "Mom, listen to this." Then she put it into the player for me to listen to. It was the gospel singer; Yolanda Adams. The song was about opening your heart to the Lord.

Once we got to the house and settled in for the night, I thought to myself, "I have to hear more of that song." It was something about the words to the song that brought conviction to my spirit. It was as though the Lord was talking directly to me. As a child growing up, I've always believed in Jesus Christ. I know that He died and rose again. But it was at this moment in time that I had my first true relationship with the Lord. I knew of Him as a child, but now I know Him for myself. When I went into the bedroom, I closed the door, I got down on my knees and listened to the song again. I began to pray. The words in the song became alive. The Lord was speaking directly to me through the words in the song.

The song went like this: alone in a room, it's just me and you, I feel so lost, I don't know what to do, what if I choose the wrong thing to do, I'm so afraid of disappointing you. I open up my heart to you.

The song spoke of everything that I was feeling inside. I wanted so desperately to get "clean." I had tried so many times before, and was never quite able to overcome the dread feeling of exhaustion that came with the first stages of trying to quit smoking crack. I wanted to do what was right. Not only just for me, but for my family.

I was ready to make a change and God knew it. I wasn't just speaking mere words. No lip service this time. You can't fool God. He knows your heart.

When I prayed; I prayed with the expectation that things would change. I prayed with hope and belief;

knowing that God would be in control of my situation; knowing that God would never leave me nor forsake me. Hallelujah, Hallelujah. For the first time in my life I experienced Hallelujah.

I didn't try to bargain with God as I had so many times in the past; back then I actually had the gall to tell God that if he would do something for me; then I would serve Him. Back then I actually believed that God needed my empty promises.

But the only thing God wanted from me was my Heart and for my yes to be yes. I surrendered to the authority of the Holy Spirit; for He performs a special work in every believer the moment that we exercise our saving faith in Christ Jesus. The Holy Spirit baptizes each believer into a union with other believers and into the Body of Christ Himself. The Holy Spirit indwells in every believer and places a seal upon every believer unto the day of redemption.

This time it was different. This time it was real. As I was on my knees praying for deliverance, I knew that the Lord would never let me fall. Only when we ask God to forgive our sins will we have true happiness and freedom from the guilt of sin.

I asked the Lord to become the landlord of my life. I said, "Lord, please; when I get back to Vallejo; take the taste of crack cocaine out of my mouth; if I smell it; please don't let it have any effect on me; if I touch it by accident- don't let it get into my pours; if I see it; let it become detestable to me; Lord please take the craving of crack cocaine away from me."

I didn't want to disappoint the Lord. When I got back to Vallejo, things were different. I was in the same environment; the same people were around me; and the same illegal activities were going on. But I was different; I had the strength of God within me this time to make the change. I had the power of Jesus Christ helping me and guiding me. My mind had been renewed. Those old behaviors were passed away. Nothing or no one could ever tempt me again. Not with crack cocaine, not with alcohol, not with any drugs; don't get me wrong, I still have problems. I get mad, I get frustrated, the same types of problems as anyone else, but those problems won't send me to jail or cause me to over-dose, or send me to eternal death.

I'm not saying that everyone should return to their old environment like I did, but this is how God dealt with me to help me through my storm. This is my testimony. He knew exactly what He was doing. I'm not saying that it was easy. With the Lord's help I dealt with it. For me; staying in that environment made me strong enough never to return to that environment again.

My calling is to go out into the community and talk with the homeless. This means that I may enter into a situation that causes me to be around people who are still using drugs. I can't have a weak mind and be easily influenced by being around an environment of people who are caught up in addiction. Maybe that's why God allowed me to stay in my old environment for so long. I stayed there maybe 6 months to a year. And I found the strength in Jesus not to use drugs, not even once.

When I got back from Visalia I was so excited about the things of God and what He did for me, I stayed in the Word all day, every day, thanks to my friend Jill who had given me a Bible. It didn't matter that I was still living in a crack house. I can do all things through Christ who strengthens me.

I picked out a room in the house; the dining room and cleaned everything in that room from top to bottom, then I wiped everything down with the blessed oil. I wrote scriptures on small pieces of paper and taped them all over the wall. The wall was full of scriptures. I had to share God's Word. I wasn't pointing out what was wrong with anyone else in the house, I was trying to explain what a filthy rag I was and how the Lord was moving in my life. Everyone that I ran into, I told them that I had been born again. I was a radical for the Lord; He is the Lord of my life and worthy to be praised. He is faithful. In His word we can depend. We can rejoice and sing praises to the Mighty King.

Through Devine Intervention, the dining room was off limits to any type of smoking; drinking; or cursing. It wasn't my house. I couldn't order anyone to do anything. I was just glade that they allowed me to have a roof over my head. Everyone was invited into the room. I explained the Blessed Oil. And everyone respected the fact that this room had been dedicated to the Lord.

In order to gain access into the kitchen, everyone would have to go through the dining room. Out of respect to the Lord, if anyone had a cigarette or a beer in their hand and needed to get into the kitchen; they would jump over the dining room and into the kitchen; sort of how a standing long jump would be in track and field. This was a beautiful jester.

Later I got news that my son John (who must have been around fifteen or sixteen years old now) was having a baseball game at Wilson Park. I borrowed a bicycle from Moosie's family; fixed it up and road it from Beverly Hills to Wilson Park. When I got there I saw my dad standing around talking to some colleagues of his; either from law enforcement or the chaplaincy program. I road my bike straight up to him; he was happy to see me. I had great news. It had been so long since I had anything as fantastic as what I was about to share and I couldn't wait.

I told my dad the news of being clean for twelve days. It was a new beginning. I remember how hard it had been just to get past that first day. If you've never been there; twelve days clean is a very long time; to me it felt like a year; and I was proud of myself; I know that I couldn't have done any of it without help from the Lord; yet I couldn't help but to be proud of myself.

To top it off my dad told me that he was proud of me too. Those four words rang out loud in my head like a bullhorn announcing victory. I felt like a gladiator in the ring holding up my sword as I placed my foot on the enemy's neck.

My dad's words gave me encouragement to keep going and to stay clean. With each new day being clean; I felt more alive. It was like being born again. I had been born again and I finally understood what that meant and I also understood how it felt.

Twelve days clean turned into fifteen days clean. Fifteen days clean turned into thirty days clean. When I got to thirty days clean; I told myself that I've got to get to sixty days clean. When I got to sixty days clean; I had to make it to six months clean.

Six months turned into one year clean. I recently celebrated 10 years of being clean and sober. 10 years of being set free and redeemed into the wonderful and glorious family of the Most High God. My re-born birthday is May 3, 2001.

God was in control of my life, as He took me through baby steps in my recovery. But knowing that He was in control and I had the assurance of his salvation; I could endure in times of trouble. I could wait patiently day by day witnessing God's grace and His goodness.

We had been working with the owner of the Arco for a couple of year now, he knew our ways and we knew his. He purchased equipment for us in the past and we were able to make a pretty good amount of money. He allowed us to wash windshield on his property. We had a good relationship with him.

After my son's baseball game; I started to think about my future. I was twelve day clean. What was I going to do with my life now? How was I going to earn money? Washing windshields was the easiest way that I knew. I'd been doing that for seven years now. The problem was I was used to using that money to buy drugs. In my mind one activity was related to the other.

Spiritually I was strong enough, but washing windshield now was going to feel different. I decided to give it a try. I went to the Arco to wash a couple of windshields with the intent of not using any drugs. When the manager saw me washing windshields he called me over to talk. He told me that he no longer wanted to see me washing windshields at his Arco any more. I was shocked; I hadn't done anything wrong that I was aware of. I really didn't know what I was going to do for money. Spiritually I was in a good place; but face it I wasn't ready to start job hunting. And I needed to eat.

Then he told me the good news. As I listened to Eradge talk; I could see the Hand of God working in and through the situation. He said that he wanted me to continue doing all of those $5 and $10 tasks; except he was going to pay me $100 per week. The only hitch was that I couldn't wash any windshields. If I did, I had to leave his establishment permanently.

You might be wondering why this would be a good thing. Well, I had my answer from the Lord. I now knew just how I was going to earn money to eat. Isn't God wonderful? A friend of mine named LeRoy once said, "You can never out give God." One hundred dollars a week might not seem like a lot to some people; but to me it was everything. The Lord blessed me abundantly. I had enough to where I knew I could eat every day; but not too much; that I might be tempted to back slide and start using drugs again. And it was enough so that I could share my food with everyone in the house. As I said before, the Lord took me through small steps -- one talent at a time.

Once when my mom was driving down the street, she said that she heard a voice coming from the back seat of her car. She knew that she was the only one in the car. She was afraid to turn around because she didn't want to have an accident. The Voice said, "I have everything under control." That voice was the Holy Spirit confirming that God is in control. The Lord has brought me from such a long way. He pulled me up and out of a dark place. He set my feet on solid ground. Never again will I walk without the Lord by my side. He is guiding me in everything that I do. If I were to turn my back on the Lord after everything that He has done for me, then I would be calling Him a liar. Because He said that He would never leave me nor forsake me. I have faith in God's Holy Word. His Word will go forth and accomplish what it says. His Word will do what it says it will do. His Word shall forever remain in me. Amen.

If you have found any inspiration in the words that I'm sharing about my life, know that deliverance is available to you. Ask the Lord right now, please do not delay; ask Him to come into your life, lead you and guide you in the path that He has prepared for your destiny; accept Jesus Christ as the Lord and Savior of your life. Remember, life in this world is a difficult journey. There will be hills to climb and valleys to fall into. In times past you gave up when things got tough. Hold onto the Lord's unchanging hand. This is your time to reap the harvest and see the salvation of the Lord unfold.

When my grandson Jason was born, I called him number eight, the number that represents new beginnings. The Lord understood me as his child and gave me a tangible gift to hold on to because He knew that's what I needed. Everyone has a gift that God has either given to you or is attempting to give to you. Please open your heart, your mind and your soul and receive the gift of eternal life.

THE BEGINNING

.

ABOUT THE AUTHOR

Robin Barnes is a mother, grandmother, daughter, sister and friend dedicated to serving God. She is over 10 years delivered from her drug addiction to crack cocaine. She now speaks when invited to churches and community organizations about her journey to recovery. She is active in her community giving hope and encouragement to those still battling drug addictions. To invite Robin Barnes for a speaking engagement, she can be contacted by e-mail at krpepper1@gmail.com.

www.ingramcontent.com/pod-product-compliance
Lightning Source LLC
Chambersburg PA
CBHW032037040426
42449CB00007B/929